Christmas Classics

Christmas Classics

Timeless recipes for the festive season

murdoch books
Sydney | London

Panforte – see page 253

Contents

'Christmas,' *penned the American writer Norman Vincent Peale,* 'weaves *a* magic wand *over this* world *and* behold, everything *is* softer *and more* beautiful.'

Let *the* festivities *begin* ...

Christmas is undeniably a time like no other and its special wonders have been much rhapsodised. Few of us can resist the sparkle of Christmas and all that it brings. We love the stirring carols sung by candlelight in community parks, the promise of a break from work and the uncontainable excitement of children as they imagine what glorious booty Santa might drop their way. We're cheered by the utter gorgeousness of tinsel, twinkling fairy lights and trees festooned with bright, fragile baubles. When December rolls around and the air is laden with seductive scents of pine needles and candy canes, everyone, it seems, is in a lovely mood. Sending cards, choosing gifts for dear ones and buying the right trimmings and treats (Christmas crackers, Christmas stockings, a wreath for the front door …) are all elements of the annual festive ritual that make Christmas special. For many of us though, it's the bringing together of family and friends around the Christmas table that holds the most allure. With the insane pace of twenty-first century life and opportunities for some relaxed consumption and uninterrupted catching-up being sadly few and far between, the shared Christmas meal is the most meaningful part of the festivities.

Unfortunately (and as we all know too well!), Christmas has a dreaded flip-side. As much as we adore the fun and feasting, there's nothing particularly magical about the stress involved in pulling off a successful Christmas Day. After all, no one wants to take short cuts at Christmas time – especially not with the food. All those scrumptious treats such as turkey, pork or venison roasts with their rich stuffings and sauces, Christmas pudding, fruit cake and mince pies, eggnog and pavlova, deserve quality ingredients and plenty of our valuable cooking time. Any cook worth their salt wants it all to look and taste perfect. But getting everything ready in time for Christmas dinner can be a logistical nightmare and it's tempting to feel overwhelmed months before December even arrives.

The best way to approach the demands of Christmas catering is *logically*, which is exactly how this book is arranged. Here, useful but wholly inspiring chapters follow the progression of a Christmas meal from first courses, main dishes, sides and desserts to puddings, party nibbles and edible gourmet gifts. Each recipe has been thoughtfully selected and rigorously tested so you can be confident of the results. There are even recipes for all those essential extras, such as gourmet gifts, confections, preserves and cocktails. This is the most useful book of Christmas recipes you'll ever own.

Before you can start thinking clearly about your Christmas cooking, you need to first decide on a menu and this can be done months in advance. Consider whether you wish to host a sit-down meal with a progression of plated courses, or a more relaxed buffet affair, where people can help themselves and graze at will. The former option is likely to involve more last-minute rustling in the kitchen on the day whereas the latter scenario has greater scope for pre-plating, leaving you freer to mingle with guests. Secure your RSVPs as far ahead as you can; once you know how many people you'll be hosting and what type of meal you'll be offering, you can begin effective planning. While you'll never completely eliminate the hard work involved in cooking a fabulous Christmas meal, by making delicious, dependable dishes from *Cooking for Christmas* and following the hints and tips throughout, you'll reduce a great deal of the potential anxiety. And that's surely a recipe for a very merry Christmas!

Tips for a *low-stress* Christmas

* When deciding on your menu, consider your budget, the type of meal (sit-down or buffet) and the number of people being catered for. To ease budget strain, buy items that will keep (dried fruits, frozen berries, wines, chocolate, liqueurs and spirits, for example) well ahead. This way, your December food bill won't be so terrifying. Similarly, select a mix of dishes that allow for an amount of pre-preparation so you can spread the workload out; some dishes can even be frozen.

* Devising your menu also requires thinking through cooking logistics – do you have enough oven space, for example, to accommodate a large piece of meat as well as the roasting vegetables, if you were considering such a scenario? If not, plan a mix of dishes that will allow you to spread the cooking load between the stovetop and oven.

* Break your Christmas menu down into its various courses then write down extensive lists of every ingredient you'll need and all the preparation tasks, from its beginning to its end. This helps organise both your thoughts *and* the workload and identifies any jobs that can be done well in advance. Ticking items off lists as ingredients are purchased, or as a job is accomplished, does wonders for your pre-Christmas sense of achievement and helps you feel supremely in control.

* Some items, such as goose, game, ham and turkey, may need to be pre-ordered so make sure you do this in good time. It is worth seeking out organic meats from a reputable butcher, as the flavour will be far superior to mass-produced alternatives. As a general guide, a 7 kilogram ham will serve around 20 people (or 10, with left-overs) and a 4.5 kilogram turkey will feed six to eight people.

* Remember you can make long-keeping items such as Christmas cake, Christmas pudding and fruit mince pies months ahead; the flavour of heavy fruit puddings and cakes actually improve over time. Store these carefully in a cool, dark place in an airtight container. Christmas cake and pudding can be wrapped in a brandy-, whisky- or rum-soaked cloth (for extra flavour and longevity) before then being wrapped completely in plastic wrap and stored as outlined above. Any special accompaniments (such as jams, pickles or chutneys) can also be made several months in advance.

* Clean out your refrigerator, freezer and pantry in early December so you know there's sufficient space available for all the extra food that will require safe storage. This is a great time to invest in some good-quality storage containers; heavy-duty plastic ones with tight-fitting lids and that stack well are space-saving and help food last longer. Zip-lock bags are also excellent for short-term storage, for using in the freezer, pantry or refrigerator. Assess whether you'll need to buy a portable ice-box and ice bricks to allow for temporary cold storage on Christmas day.

* Consider having your knives professionally sharpened if their edges are dull. Alternatively, using an electric knife is the best way to make short work of all that laborious Christmas carving and slicing, and these are not terribly expensive to buy.

* One week before Christmas is the ideal time to make shortbread, rocky road, rum and raisin balls, gingerbread, panforte, frozen desserts and those other essential sweet treats. Savoury biscuits, nut mixes and flavoured butters can also be made now. Many of these items will keep well in airtight containers while others can be frozen until Christmas Eve or Christmas morning. Stock to be used as the base for soups and sauces, plus toasts and pastries can also be made now – these will freeze. You can even roll out your pastry and freeze it, lined inside baking tins, so it is ready to blind bake or fill.

* Several days before Christmas, make terrines, brandy butter, glazes for ham, stuffings and any vegetable dishes or soups that will successfully reheat. Mayonnaises, rillettes, cocktail bases, custards and ice cubes should also be made now and cakes should be iced; if the load is daunting, spread the cooking over 2 or 3 days.

* The day before Christmas is the day to chill your drinks, polish glassware and cutlery, iron napery, pick up flowers, fresh fruits, salad greens and vegetables and any other last-minute goodies. Vegetables for roasting can be trimmed and chopped and stored overnight in zip-lock bags in the refrigerator. Green leaves for salads can be washed, spun dry and stored in zip lock bags in the refrigerator too. Fragile desserts such as pavlova, and other dishes that don't last well should also be made now.

* By the time Christmas Day swings around, most of the large jobs should be done but those that are left (roasting or glazing meat, making dressings and gravy, cooking vegetable dishes, tossing salads, whipping cream, heating puddings etc) still require careful planning and some precision timing. Make sure you have a few pairs of willing hands to help with all the last-minute preparations … and with the clean-up too.

JOYE

First course

Heighten anticipation of the main meal with elegant and simple dishes that set the scene for a Christmas feast to remember.

French onion *soup*

SERVES *6*
PREPARATION TIME *20 minutes*
COOKING TIME *1 hour*

50 G (1¾ OZ) *butter*
740 G (1 LB 10 OZ) *onions,* FINELY SLICED
2 *garlic cloves,* CRUSHED
40 G (1½ OZ/⅓ CUP) *plain (all-purpose) flour*
2 LITRES (70 FL OZ/8 CUPS) *beef or chicken stock*
250 ML (9 FL OZ/1 CUP) *dry white wine*
1 *bay leaf*
2 *thyme sprigs*
12 SLICES DAY-OLD *baguette*
100 G (3½ OZ) *grûyère cheese,* FINELY GRATED

Melt the butter in a saucepan over low heat, add the onion and cook, stirring occasionally, for 25 minutes, or until the onion is deep golden brown and beginning to caramelise.

Add the garlic and flour and stir continuously for 2 minutes. Slowly stir in the stock and wine and bring to the boil. Add the bay leaf and thyme, season with sea salt and freshly ground black pepper, then cover the pan and simmer for 25 minutes. Remove the herbs and check the seasoning.

Preheat the grill (broiler) to medium.

Toast the baguette slices, divide among six warmed soup bowls, then ladle the soup over the top. Sprinkle with the grated cheese and place the bowls under the grill until the cheese melts and turns light golden brown.

Spiced pumpkin *soup* *with* ginger cream

SERVES *4–6*
PREPARATION TIME *20 minutes*
COOKING TIME *30 minutes*

1 TEASPOON *cumin seeds*
1 TABLESPOON *olive oil*
1 *onion,* FINELY CHOPPED
1 *garlic clove,* CRUSHED
1 TEASPOON *grated fresh ginger*
1 TEASPOON *cumin*
1 TEASPOON *ground coriander*
1/4 TEASPOON *dried chilli flakes*
750 G (1 LB 10 OZ) *pumpkin (winter squash),* CHOPPED
1 LITRE (35 FL OZ/4 CUPS) *vegetable stock*
100 G (3 1/2 OZ) PIECE *speck,* SLICED INTO THIN STRIPS
1 TABLESPOON FINELY CHOPPED *coriander (cilantro) leaves*

Ginger cream

90 G (3 1/4 OZ/1/3 CUP) *sour cream*
80 ML (2 1/2 FL OZ/1/3 CUP) *cream (whipping)*
1 TEASPOON GRATED *fresh ginger*
1 TEASPOON *lemon juice*
1 TABLESPOON FINELY CHOPPED *coriander (cilantro) leaves*

Place the cumin seeds in a small frying pan and cook over medium heat until fragrant. Crush using a mortar and pestle until finely ground.

Heat the oil in a large saucepan, add the onion and cook over medium heat for 2 minutes, or until just soft. Add the garlic, ginger, cumin, ground coriander and chilli flakes and cook, stirring constantly, until fragrant. Add the pumpkin and stock and bring to the boil. Reduce the heat to low and simmer, uncovered, for 20 minutes, or until the pumpkin is tender.

Meanwhile, fry the speck in a small frying pan over high heat until golden brown and crisp.

To make the ginger cream, combine the sour cream, cream, ginger and lemon juice in a small bowl and beat until slightly thickened. Fold in the coriander.

Blend or process the soup until smooth. Return the soup to the cleaned saucepan and reheat gently over low heat. Ladle into serving bowls and top with a dollop of ginger cream, a sprinkle of coriander and a few pieces of speck.

Beetroot *salad* *with* goat's cheese

SERVES *6*
PREPARATION TIME *20 minutes*
COOKING TIME *1 hour and 10 minutes*

1½ TABLESPOONS *olive oil*
4 MEDIUM *beetroot (beets),* SCRUBBED
125 ML (4 FL OZ/½ CUP) *red wine*
2 TABLESPOONS *red wine vinegar*
2 TABLESPOONS *soft brown sugar*
8 *cloves*
120 G (4¼ OZ) *goat's cheese*
125 ML (4 FL OZ/½ CUP) *cream (whipping)*
thyme leaves, TO SERVE
toasted brioche, TO SERVE

Preheat the oven to 220°C (425°F/Gas 7).

Lightly rub 1 tablespoon of the oil into the beetroot. Wrap the beetroot in foil, place on a large baking tray and roast for 1 hour, or until tender when pierced with a skewer. Remove from the oven and allow to cool slightly. Peel and thinly slice using a sharp knife or mandolin.

Combine the wine, vinegar, sugar and cloves in a saucepan over medium–high heat and bring to the boil. Reduce the heat to low and simmer for 5 minutes, or until slightly syrupy. Remove from the heat, add the beetroot and allow to cool.

Meanwhile, place the cheese and cream in a bowl and beat using electric beaters until pale and fluffy, about 3 minutes.

Drain the beetroot, reserving the liquid. Whisk 60 ml (2 fl oz/¼ cup) of the reserved beetroot poaching liquid with the remaining oil.

Divide the beetroot between six serving plates, slightly overlapping the slices, and dot with the whipped goat's cheese. Drizzle on the dressing and scatter with the thyme leaves. Serve with the toasted brioche.

Champagne *risotto*

SERVES *6*
PREPARATION TIME *15 minutes*
COOKING TIME *25 minutes*

500 ML (17 FL OZ/2 CUPS) *chicken stock*
40 G (1½ OZ) *butter*
2 *French shallots,* FINELY CHOPPED
220 G (7¾ OZ/1 CUP) *vialone nano* OR *other risotto rice*
200 ML (7 FL OZ) *Champagne* OR *sparkling white wine*
75 G (2¾ OZ/⅓ CUP) *mascarpone cheese*
60 ML (2 FL OZ/¼ CUP) *cream*
25 G (1 OZ/¼ CUP) FINELY GRATED *parmesan cheese*
1½ TEASPOONS CHOPPED *tarragon*
½ *white truffle* OR ½ *black truffle,* SHAVED (OPTIONAL)

Combine the stock and 500 ml (17 fl oz/2 cups) water in a saucepan, bring to the boil and reduce the heat to a gentle simmer.

Meanwhile, melt the butter in a large saucepan over medium heat. Add the shallot and cook, stirring occasionally, for 5 minutes, or until softened. Add the rice and stir for 1–2 minutes, or until the rice is lightly toasted. Add the Champagne or sparkling wine and stir until absorbed. Add enough of the hot stock to barely cover the rice and cook, stirring constantly, until the liquid is almost completely absorbed. Continue adding the stock, a little at a time, until all the stock is absorbed and the rice is al dente, about 18 minutes. Remove from the heat, cover and allow to stand for 3 minutes.

Combine the mascarpone, cream, parmesan and tarragon in a small saucepan over low heat and cook for 5 minutes, or until slightly reduced.

Divide the risotto among serving plates and drizzle with the mascarpone cream. Season with sea salt and freshly ground black pepper, scatter over slices of the truffle and serve.

Gravlax *with* horseradish *cream*

SERVES *8–10*
PREPARATION TIME *20 minutes, plus 24–48 hours chilling time*

900 G (2 LB) SIDE OF *salmon,* SKIN ON, BONES REMOVED
2 TABLESPOONS *gin*
1 TEASPOON *black peppercorns,* LIGHTLY CRUSHED
2 TEASPOONS *juniper berries,* LIGHTLY CRUSHED
60 G (2¼ OZ) *rock salt*
60 G (2¼ OZ) *sugar*
4 TABLESPOONS FINELY CHOPPED *dill*
FINELY GRATED ZEST OF 1 *lemon*
rye bread, TO SERVE

Dill and horseradish cream

150 G (5½ OZ) *sour cream*
1½ TABLESPOONS FRESHLY GRATED *horseradish*
2 TABLESPOONS *lemon juice*
2 TABLESPOONS FINELY CHOPPED *dill*

Line a baking tray with plastic wrap, allowing for plenty of overhang to completely wrap the salmon.

Place the salmon, skin side down, on the prepared tray and rub the gin into the flesh.

Combine the peppercorns, juniper berries, salt, sugar, dill and lemon zest in a bowl, mix well and press onto the salmon. Fold the plastic wrap around the salmon to seal. Refrigerate for 24–48 hours, turning every 12 hours.

To make the dill and horseradish cream, place the sour cream, horseradish, lemon juice and dill in a bowl and mix to combine.

Unwrap the salmon and scrape off the salt mixture. Very thinly slice the salmon across the grain on a slight angle. Serve with the rye bread and the dill and horseradish cream.

Jerusalem artichoke *and* chestnut *soup*

SERVES *8*
PREPARATION TIME *20 minutes*
COOKING TIME *1 hour and 20 minutes*

350 G (12 OZ) FRESH *chestnuts*
1.25 KG (2 LB 12 OZ) *jerusalem artichokes,* PEELED AND CHOPPED
2 TABLESPOONS *olive oil*
1 *onion,* FINELY CHOPPED
2 *garlic cloves,* CRUSHED
1 *boiling potato,* PEELED AND CHOPPED
2 LITRES (70 FL OZ/8 CUPS) *chicken stock*
50 G (1¾ OZ) *butter,* SOFTENED
90 ML (3 FL OZ) *cream*

Preheat the oven to 180°C (350°F/Gas 4).

Score a small cross on the base of each chestnut and place on a baking tray. Bake for 20–25 minutes, or until the skins start to split. Wrap the chestnuts in a tea towel (dish towel), leave for 5 minutes, then peel, one at a time, removing the outer and inner skin. Set aside to cool, then finely chop.

Place the artichokes on a baking tray, drizzle with 1 tablespoon of the oil, season with sea salt and bake for 30 minutes, or until lightly coloured.

Heat the remaining oil in a saucepan over low heat and cook the onion and garlic for 5 minutes, or until soft. Add the artichoke, potato and stock and simmer for 20 minutes, or until the potato and artichoke are soft. Add the butter and cream, stir to combine and simmer gently for 1 minute. Allow to cool slightly and blend, in batches, until smooth. Return the soup to the cleaned saucepan and reheat over low heat. Season with sea salt and freshly ground black pepper and serve sprinkled with the toasted chestnuts.

Potted prawns *with* Melba *toasts*

SERVES *6*
PREPARATION TIME *20 minutes, plus 3 hours chilling time*
COOKING TIME *5 minutes, plus cooling time*

1.8 KG (4 LB) *raw large prawns (shrimp),* PEELED AND DEVEINED
50 G (1¾ OZ) *unsalted butter*
2 TEASPOONS *sea salt*
60 ML (2 FL OZ/¼ CUP) *thick cream*
2 TABLESPOONS ROUGHLY CHOPPED *tarragon*
1 TABLESPOON *lemon juice*
2 TABLESPOONS FINELY SNIPPED *chives*
Melba toasts, TO SERVE
FRESHLY CHOPPED *flat-leaf (Italian) parsley,* TO GARNISH

Lightly grease six 125 ml (4 fl oz/½ cup) ramekins and set aside.

Place the prawns in the bowl of a food processor and pulse in short bursts until roughly chopped.

Melt the butter in a large saucepan over medium heat. Add the prawns and salt and cook, stirring occasionally, for 3 minutes, or until the prawns are just cooked through. Remove from the heat and stir in the cream, tarragon, lemon juice, and chives.

Divide the prawn mixture between the prepared ramekins and press down to remove any air bubbles. Allow to cool, cover with plastic wrap and chill in the refrigerator for 3 hours, or until set. Garnish the potted prawns with the parsley and serve with the Melba toasts.

Smoked duck breast *with* celeriac *and* fennel *remoulade*

SERVES *8*
PREPARATION TIME *15 minutes*
COOKING TIME *35 minutes, plus resting time*

20 G (3/4 OZ/1/4 CUP) *black tea leaves*
95 G (3 1/4 OZ/1/2 CUP) *jasmine rice*
2 TABLESPOONS *soft brown sugar*
2 *star anise*
2 *cinnamon sticks*
4 *duck breasts,* ABOUT 220 G (7 3/4 OZ) EACH, SKIN SCORED

Lemon mayonnaise

2 *egg yolks*
1 TEASPOON *dijon mustard*
1 1/2 TABLESPOONS *lemon juice*
1 TEASPOON FINELY GRATED *lemon zest*
300 ML (10 1/2 FL OZ) *vegetable oil*

Celeriac and fennel remoulade

1 SMALL *celeriac,* ABOUT 350 G (12 OZ), PEELED
1 LARGE *fennel bulb,* ABOUT 400 G (14 OZ)
2 TABLESPOONS *salted baby capers,* DRAINED, RINSED AND CHOPPED
2 TABLESPOONS FINELY CHOPPED *chervil*
2 TABLESPOONS FINELY CHOPPED *flat-leaf (Italian) parsley*

Line a baking tray with foil. Cover a wire rack with baking paper.

To make the lemon mayonnaise, place the egg yolks, mustard, lemon juice and lemon zest in the bowl of a food processor and pulse for 30 seconds. With the motor running, gradually add the oil in a thin steady stream and process until well combined and the mayonnaise is thick and creamy. Refrigerate until required.

To make the celeriac and fennel remoulade, cut the celeriac and fennel into thin matchsticks 4.5 cm (1 3/4 inches) long. Combine the celeriac, fennel, capers, chervil, parsley and lemon mayonnaise in a large bowl and mix well.

Meanwhile, combine the tea leaves, rice, sugar, star anise and cinnamon sticks in a bowl and mix well. Transfer to the prepared tray, spreading the smoking mixture evenly over the base. Place the covered wire rack over the smoking mixture and cover with another baking tray of the same size or securely tuck a sheet of foil around the edges of the tray to keep in the smoke. Preheat the smoking tray on two gas burners over low–medium heat for 10 minutes.

Heat a large frying pan over medium heat. Add the duck, skin side down, and cook for 10 minutes, or until the skin is golden and crisp. Transfer the duck to the wire rack in the smoking tray, cover tightly and cook for 15 minutes, or until the duck is just pink in the centre. Remove the duck, loosely cover with foil and set aside in a warm place to rest for 5 minutes. Slice on a slight angle.

Divide the celeriac and fennel remoulade between eight plates and top each with slices of duck breast.

Game *terrine*

SERVES *10*
PREPARATION TIME *30 minutes, plus overnight chilling time*
COOKING TIME *55 minutes*

310 G (11 OZ) *duck, squab or guinea fowl meat,* COARSELY MINCED (GROUND)
200 G (7 OZ) *pork shoulder,* COARSELY MINCED (GROUND)
230 G (8¼ OZ) *pork back fat,* COARSELY MINCED (GROUND)
1 TABLESPOON *Cognac*
1 TABLESPOON *Madeira*
2 TABLESPOONS *chicken stock*
1 *egg yolk*
½ TEASPOON FINELY GRATED *orange zest*
2 TABLESPOONS *pistachio nuts*
½ TEASPOON CHOPPED *thyme*
1 *garlic clove,* CRUSHED
2 TEASPOONS *salt*
½ TEASPOON FRESHLY *ground black pepper*
PINCH OF *quatre-épices*
PINCH OF FRESHLY GRATED *nutmeg*
1 *juniper berry,* CRUSHED
PINCH OF GROUND *ginger*
10 SLICES *prosciutto*
2 *bay leaves*
toasted brioche, TO SERVE

Preheat the oven to 120°C (235°F/Gas ½). Line a 24 x 7.5 cm (9½ x 3 inch) terrine tin with two layers of plastic wrap, making sure there is plenty of overhang.

Line the base and sides of the terrine tin with the prosciutto, overlapping the slices slightly and allowing them to overhang the two long edges of the tin. Spoon in the duck mixture and press firmly into the sides and corners. Smooth the surface and fold the overhanging prosciutto over the filling. Place the bay leaves on top and cover with the overhanging plastic wrap.

Combine the duck, squab or guinea fowl, the pork shoulder and pork fat in a large mixing bowl, add the Cognac, Madeira, stock, egg yolk, orange zest, pistachio nuts, thyme, garlic, salt, pepper and spices and mix well.

Place the terrine in a roasting tin. Fill the roasting tin with boiling water to come halfway up the sides of the terrine tin. Bake for 55 minutes, or until the juices run clear when a skewer is inserted in the centre of the terrine. Remove the terrine from the roasting tin and refrigerate overnight. Cut into slices and serve with the brioche.

Seared scallops *with* lemon butter *and* herbs

SERVES *6*
PREPARATION TIME *10 minutes*
COOKING TIME *5 minutes*

18 *scallops,* ON THE SHELL
60 G (2¼ OZ/¼ CUP) *unsalted butter,* CHOPPED
FINELY GRATED ZEST OF ½ *lemon*
2 TABLESPOONS *lemon juice*
1 TABLESPOON *olive oil*
1½ TABLESPOONS FINELY CHOPPED *flat-leaf (Italian) parsley*

Remove the scallops from their shells using a sharp knife. Rinse and dry the shells.

Melt the butter in a small saucepan over low heat, add the lemon zest and juice and stir to combine.

Heat a non-stick frying pan over high heat, add the oil and sear the scallops, in two batches, for 30 seconds on each side, or until golden, adding a little more oil if necessary. Remove from the pan and place on the prepared shells, drizzle with some lemon butter and top with the parsley.

Red lentil, ham *and* sage *soup*

SERVES *8–10*
PREPARATION TIME *35 minutes*
COOKING TIME *2 hours and 15 minutes*

1 TABLESPOON *olive oil*
3 *red onions,* FINELY CHOPPED
2 *large celery stalks,* FINELY CHOPPED
2 *large carrots,* FINELY CHOPPED
4 *garlic cloves,* CHOPPED
1 TABLESPOON FINELY CHOPPED *coriander (cilantro) root*
10 G (¼ OZ) *sage,* CHOPPED
1 *ham hock,* CUT INTO 4 THICK SLICES (ASK YOUR BUTCHER TO DO THIS)
1 *sweet potato,* (KUMARA) ABOUT 500 G (1 LB 2 OZ), PEELED AND CHOPPED INTO 2 CM (¾ INCH) DICE
2 *bay leaves*
250 G (9 OZ/1 CUP) *red lentils,* RINSED
220 G (7¾ OZ/1 CUP) *pearl barley*
1 *large tomato,* FINELY CHOPPED
crusty bread, TO SERVE

Heat the oil in a large saucepan over medium heat, add the onion, celery, carrot, garlic, coriander and sage and cook, stirring occasionally, for 6–8 minutes, or until the vegetables are soft. Add the ham hock, sweet potato, bay leaves, lentils, barley, tomato and 3 litres (105 fl oz/12 cups) cold water and bring to the boil. Partially cover and simmer for 1½–2 hours, stirring occasionally and skimming to remove impurities.

Place half the soup in the bowl of a food processor and process until smooth. Return to the pan, remove the ham hocks from the soup and take the meat off the bones. Add the trimmed meat only back into the soup and gently reheat the soup. Season to taste and serve with some crusty bread.

Mushroom *pithiviers*

SERVES *6*
PREPARATION TIME *25 minutes, plus 10 minutes soaking time*
COOKING TIME *45 minutes, plus cooling time*

10 G (¼ OZ) DRIED *porcini mushrooms*
60 ML (2 FL OZ/¼ CUP) *boiling water*
30 G (1 OZ) *butter*
1 *leek,* WHITE PART ONLY, THINLY SLICED
300 G (10½ OZ) *mixed mushrooms,* SUCH AS OYSTER, SWISS BROWN, ENOKI, SLICED
1 TEASPOON CHOPPED *rosemary*
80 ML (2½ FL OZ/⅓ CUP) *Madeira*
1 TEASPOON *cornflour (cornstarch)*
60 ML (2 FL OZ/¼ CUP) *cream*
2 TABLESPOONS FINELY CHOPPED *flat-leaf (Italian) parsley*
3 SHEETS *frozen butter puff pastry,* THAWED
1 *egg,* LIGHTLY BEATEN
watercress sprigs, TO SERVE

Place the porcini in a small bowl, cover with the boiling water and allow to stand for 10 minutes, or until the mushrooms have softened. Drain the mushrooms, reserving the soaking liquid, and coarsely chop.

Melt the butter in a large frying pan over low–medium heat. Add the leek and cook, stirring occasionally, for 5 minutes, or until soft. Increase the heat to high, add the mushrooms and rosemary and cook, stirring occasionally, for 7 minutes, or until the mushrooms have wilted. Add the Madeira and cook for 2 minutes, or until the Madeira has evaporated.

Combine the reserved porcini soaking liquid and the cornflour in a small bowl and stir until smooth.

Add the cornflour mixture and the cream to the mushrooms and cook, stirring occasionally, for 3 minutes, or until slightly thickened. Season to taste and stir in the parsley. Set aside to cool.

Preheat the oven to 220°C (425°F/Gas 7). Then line a baking tray with baking paper.

Cut twelve 12 cm (4½ inch) rounds from the butter puff pastry. Place 2 tablespoons of the mushroom mixture on half the rounds, spreading the filling to 1 cm (½ inch) from the edge of the pastry. Lightly brush the egg around the edge of the pastry. Place the remaining pastry rounds on top and seal the edges to enclose the filling. Transfer to the prepared tray and brush the tops with the remaining egg. Bake for 20–25 minutes, or until puffed and golden.

Roast baby beetroot, fennel *and* mozzarella *salad*

SERVES *4–6*
PREPARATION TIME *20 minutes*
COOKING TIME *50 minutes, plus cooling time*

12 *baby beetroot (beets),* STEMS TRIMMED
1 TABLESPOON *olive oil*
1 *curly endive,* TRIMMED
2 *baby fennel bulbs,* TRIMMED AND THINLY SLICED LENGTHWAYS
2 *blood oranges,* SEGMENTED
2 *buffalo mozzarella,* TORN INTO BITE-SIZED PIECES
2 TABLESPOONS *hazelnuts* OR *pistachio nuts,* TOASTED, SKINNED AND CHOPPED

Mustard lemon dressing

2 TABLESPOONS *olive oil*
1 TABLESPOON *lemon juice*
1 TEASPOON *dijon mustard*
1 TEASPOON *honey*

To make the mustard lemon dressing, whisk the oil, lemon juice, mustard and honey in a small bowl. Season with sea salt and freshly ground black pepper.

Preheat the oven to 180°C (350°F/Gas 4). Line a baking tray with baking paper.

Wash the beetroot and pat dry with paper towel. Place on the prepared tray and drizzle on the oil to lightly coat. Bake for 40–50 minutes, or until tender when pierced with a fork. Allow to cool, rub off the skin and cut in half. Place the beetroot in a bowl and add enough of the dressing to moisten. Set aside.

Arrange the endive on a large platter. Scatter over the fennel, orange and mozzarella. Scatter on the beetroot and nuts, drizzle over the remaining dressing and serve at once.

TIP: If preparing the fennel in advance, place the slices in a bowl of acidulated water to stop browning. Drain and pat dry with paper towel just before serving.

Crab bisque *with* herb oil

SERVES *6*
PREPARATION TIME *20 minutes*
COOKING TIME *55 minutes*

2 *live crabs,* ABOUT 1 KG (2 LB 4 OZ) EACH
1 *leek,* WHITE PART ONLY, ROUGHLY CHOPPED
2 *carrots,* ROUGHLY CHOPPED
2 *celery stalks,* ROUGHLY CHOPPED
1 *garlic clove,* CRUSHED
1 *bay leaf*
20 G (3/4 OZ) *unsalted butter*
1 *fennel bulb,* TRIMMED AND FINELY DICED
2 TABLESPOONS *tomato paste (concentrated purée)*
100 ML (3 1/2 FL OZ) *brandy* OR *dry white wine*
200 ML (7 FL OZ) *cream*

Herb oil

50 G (1 3/4 OZ) *chives,* SNIPPED
150 G (5 1/2 OZ) *flat-leaf (Italian) parsley*
200 ML (7 FL OZ) *olive oil*

Place the crabs in the freezer for 1 hour.

Meanwhile, to make the herb oil, bring a saucepan of water to the boil, add the herbs and blanch for 30 seconds. Drain and place the herbs in a clean tea towel (dish towel), tightly rolling it up to remove any excess liquid. Place the herbs and the oil in the bowl of a food processor and process until they are well combined.

Place the leek, carrot, celery, garlic and bay leaf in a large saucepan, add 4 litres (140 fl oz/16 cups) water and bring to the boil. Reduce to a simmer, add the crabs and cook for 12–15 minutes, or until the crab shells turn orange. Remove the crabs from the stock and set aside to cool. When the crabs are cool enough to handle, remove all the crabmeat and set aside.

Return the shells to the stock, bring to the boil and cook over high heat for 20 minutes, or until reduced by half. Reduce the heat to low so that the stock returns to simmering point and skim any impurities from the top. Remove from the heat and strain the stock into a jug, discarding the shells and vegetables.

Melt the butter in a large saucepan over medium heat, add the fennel and cook, stirring occasionally, for 3–4 minutes, or until softened. Stir in the tomato paste and cook for 1 minute. Add the brandy or wine and the reserved stock and bring to the boil. Reduce the heat to low and simmer for 10 minutes. Whisk in the cream and simmer gently for 1 minute to warm through.

Divide the crabmeat between six serving bowls, pour over the hot bisque and drizzle with the herb oil.

Bitter greens salad *with* *pickled* prawns

SERVES *6*
PREPARATION TIME *20 minutes, plus 1 hour marinating time*
COOKING TIME *5 minutes*

185 ML (6 FL OZ/3/4 CUP) *verjuice*
2 TABLESPOONS *caster (superfine) sugar*
1 *bay leaf*
1 *Lebanese (short) cucumber,* SEEDED AND FINELY DICED
1/2 *red onion,* FINELY CHOPPED
900 G (2 LB) COOKED *tiger prawns (shrimp),* PEELED AND DEVEINED, LEAVING THE TAIL INTACT
50 G (1 3/4 OZ) *mizuna*
50 G (1 3/4 OZ) *baby rocket (arugula)*
1/2 HEAD *radicchio,* LEAVES TORN
2 TABLESPOONS *extra virgin olive oil*

Combine the verjuice, sugar and bay leaf in a small saucepan and simmer over medium heat for 2 minutes, stirring to dissolve the sugar. Remove from the heat and set aside to cool.

Place the cucumber, onion and prawns in a non-metallic bowl. Add the verjuice mixture, stir well, cover and refrigerate for 1 hour.

Place the salad leaves in a serving bowl. Remove the prawns from the marinade and toss with the leaves. Combine the oil and 60 ml (2 fl oz/1/4 cup) of the marinade in a small bowl, season to taste and then drizzle over the salad.

Braised quail *with* grapes, honey *and* sage

SERVES *6*
PREPARATION TIME *20 minutes, plus 3–4 hours marinating time*
COOKING TIME *20 minutes*

3 LARGE *quail*
3 x 5 CM (2 INCH) STRIPS OF *orange zest*
2 TABLESPOONS FINELY CHOPPED *sage*
1 *garlic clove,* CRUSHED
½ TEASPOON *sea salt*
60 G (2¼ OZ/¼ CUP) *unsalted butter*
1 TABLESPOON *olive oil*
500 ML (17 FL OZ/2 CUPS) *chicken stock*
100 ML (3½ FL OZ) *verjuice*
1 TABLESPOON *honey*
250 G (9 OZ) LARGE *seedless green grapes*
200 G (7 OZ) *curly endive*
50 G (1¾ OZ/⅓ CUP) *pine nuts,* TOASTED, TO SERVE
sage leaves, TO SERVE

Halve the quail, cutting through the backbone and breastbone. Rinse and pat dry with paper towel.

Pound the orange zest, sage, garlic and salt using a mortar and pestle until bruised and crushed. Rub the marinade mixture into the quail and place in a ceramic dish. Cover and refrigerate for 3–4 hours.

Brush the marinade mixture off the quail and reserve. Heat the butter and oil in a flameproof casserole dish over medium–high heat. Add the quail, skin side down, and cook for 1–2 minutes on each side, or until brown. Pour in the stock, verjuice, honey and reserved marinade mixture. Cover with a lid, bring to a simmer and cook for 10–12 minutes, or until the quail is just cooked through.

Remove the quail and keep warm. Strain the cooking liquid through a fine sieve into a small saucepan, discarding the solids. Place the pan over medium–high heat and bring to a simmer. Add the grapes and simmer for 2 minutes, or until warmed through and the grape skins begin to split.

Arrange a bed of endive leaves on each serving plate and place a quail half on top. Drizzle over the sauce and grapes, scatter on the pine nuts and garnish with the sage leaves.

Main course

With this fine offering of traditional favourites and more contemporary dishes, there's something the whole family can enjoy.

Roast turkey *with* hazelnut *and* porcini *stuffing*

SERVES *10–12*
PREPARATION TIME *30 minutes*
COOKING TIME *4 hours, plus cooling and resting time*

7 KG (15 LB 12 OZ) *turkey*
1 QUANTITY *hazelnut and porcini stuffing* (PAGE 95)
50 G ($1^{3}/_{4}$ OZ) *butter,* SOFTENED
750 ML (26 FL OZ/3 CUPS) *chicken stock*
40 G ($1^{1}/_{2}$ OZ/$^{1}/_{3}$ CUP) *plain (all-purpose) flour*
ROASTED *balsamic onions* (PAGE 113)
Cherry sauce (PAGE 99)

Garlic butter

1 *garlic bulb*
200 G (7 OZ) *butter,* SOFTENED
1 TABLESPOON FINELY CHOPPED *flat-leaf (Italian) parsley*
1 TABLESPOON FINELY CHOPPED *sage*
1 TABLESPOON *lemon juice*

To make the garlic butter, break the cloves from the garlic bulb and place in a small saucepan. Cover with water, bring to the boil and simmer for 10 minutes. Allow to cool, then slip the garlic flesh from the skins. Place the garlic in a small bowl and mash with the butter. Stir in the parsley, sage and lemon juice, season and set aside.

Remove all but the bottom shelf from the oven. Preheat the oven to 200°C (400°F/Gas 6). Remove the giblets and neck from the turkey and place them in a large roasting tin. Rinse the turkey and pat dry with paper towel. Place a rack in the tin and sit the turkey on top. Spoon the stuffing into the cavity, ensuring it is only loosely packed. Starting at the neck, carefully work the skin away from the breast by sliding your hand between the skin and flesh. Carefully spread the garlic butter under the skin, ensuring that the whole breast area is well covered. Rub the butter all over the turkey and season. Loosely tie the legs together with kitchen string and cover the bird (but not the whole roasting tin) with foil.

Pour the stock into the base of the tin. Roast for 1 hour, basting with the pan juices halfway through. Reduce the temperature to 190°C (375°F/Gas 5) and roast for 2 hours and 20 minutes, basting every 30 minutes or so. Remove the foil and roast for a further 40 minutes, or until the turkey is golden and the juices run clear when a skewer is inserted into the thickest part of the thigh.

Lift the turkey onto a serving platter, cover loosely with foil and set aside to rest in a warm place for 25 minutes. Strain the juices from the roasting tin into a large jug and set aside for 10 minutes to allow them to settle. Place the tin over medium–high heat and transfer 2 tablespoons of fat from the top of the juices to the tin. Add enough water to the jug to make 750 ml (26 fl oz/3 cups). Sprinkle the flour over base of the tin and stir, scraping up the residue, for 1 minute. Gradually stir in the stock and simmer for 8–10 minutes to make a smooth gravy. Season well. Carve the turkey and serve with the stuffing and the gravy, balsamic onions and cherry sauce.

Glazed *ham*

SERVES *12*
PREPARATION TIME *10 minutes*
COOKING TIME *1 hour and 5 minutes, plus resting time*

6 KG (13 LB 8 OZ) COOKED *leg of ham*
70 G (2½ OZ/½ CUP) *cloves*

Orange glaze

250 ML (9 FL OZ/1 CUP) FRESHLY SQUEEZED *orange juice*
140 G (5 OZ/¾ CUP) *soft brown sugar*
1 TABLESPOON *dijon mustard*
175 G (6 OZ/½ CUP) *honey*
2 TEASPOONS *soy sauce*
2 TABLESPOONS *Grand Marnier*

OR

Mustard and redcurrant glaze

90 G (3¼ OZ/⅓ CUP) *dijon mustard*
315 G (11 OZ/1 CUP) *redcurrant jelly*
4 *garlic cloves,* CRUSHED
2 TABLESPOONS *vegetable oil*
2 TABLESPOONS *soy sauce*

Preheat the oven to 200°C (400°F/Gas 6).

Choose your favourite glaze.

To make the orange glaze, combine the orange juice, sugar, mustard, honey, soy sauce and Grand Marnier in a bowl and mix well.

To make the mustard and redcurrant glaze, place the mustard, redcurrant jelly, garlic, oil and soy sauce in a small saucepan over medium heat and cook, stirring occasionally, for 2–3 minutes, or until the jelly has melted. Take care that the glaze doesn't catch on the base of the pan.

Use a small sharp knife to cut through the rind around the shank of the ham. To remove the rind, run your thumb around the edge of the cut, under the rind, then ease your hand in between the rind and fat and carefully lift the rind from the fat in one piece. (Keep the rind and use it to cover the cut ham when storing.)

Score diagonal cuts into the fat at 4 cm (1½ inch) intervals, forming a diamond pattern. Do not cut all the way through to the ham or the fat will fall off during cooking. Spread half the glaze of your choice over the ham with a palette knife or the back of a spoon and press a clove into the centre of each diamond.

Place the ham, fat side up, on a rack in a roasting tin and pour 500 ml (17 fl oz/2 cups) water into the roasting tin. Cover the ham and roasting tin securely with greased foil and bake for 30–40 minutes. Remove from the oven and brush or spread the remaining glaze over the ham. Increase the oven temperature to 210°C (415°F/Gas 6–7) and bake, uncovered, for 20 minutes, or until the surface is lightly caramelised and the ham is golden brown. Set aside for 15 minutes to rest before carving.

TIP: Carving the ham is easier if you hold onto the unglazed shank end.

Rosemary pork rack *with* pear purée

SERVES *6*
PREPARATION TIME *20 minutes*
COOKING TIME *2 hours and 20 minutes, plus resting time*

6-rib standing rack of pork, ABOUT 2 KG (4 LB 8 OZ)
2 TABLESPOONS *olive oil*
2 TEASPOONS ROUGHLY CHOPPED *rosemary*
1 TABLESPOON *sea salt*
1 *onion,* THICKLY SLICED
5 *rosemary sprigs*
4 *beurre bosc pears,* PEELED AND QUARTERED
80 ML (2½ FL OZ/⅓ CUP) *port*
½ TEASPOON FINELY CHOPPED *rosemary*
375 ML (13 FL OZ/1½ CUPS) *chicken stock*

Preheat the oven to 230°C (450°F/Gas 8).

Score the rind of the pork with a sharp knife (or ask your butcher to do this for you).

Combine the oil, roughly chopped rosemary and salt in a small bowl, then smear all over the pork, rubbing well into the rind. Scatter the onion and four of the rosemary sprigs over the base of a roasting tin and place the pork on top. Roast for 20 minutes, then remove from the oven.

Arrange the pears around the base of the pork, return to the oven and roast for a further 1¾–2 hours, or until the juices run clear when the thickest part of the meat is pierced with a skewer. Remove the pork from the tin, cover with foil and set aside to rest in a warm place.

Meanwhile, to make the pear purée, blend all but six quarters of the pears until smooth. Set aside and keep warm.

To make the rosemary jus, drain off all but 2 tablespoons of the juices in the roasting tin. Place the tin over medium heat, add the port and scrape up all the sediment in the base of the tin. Add the remaining rosemary sprig and the stock, bring to the boil, reduce the heat to low and simmer for 5 minutes, or until reduced to 185 ml (6 fl oz/¾ cup). Strain, stir in the finely chopped rosemary and season to taste.

Slice the pork into individual cutlets and serve with a spoonful of the warm pear purée, a baked pear quarter and a drizzle of the rosemary jus.

Spatchcocks *with* marmalade *and* whisky *sauce*

SERVES *6*
PREPARATION TIME *15 minutes*
COOKING TIME *1 hour, plus resting time*

250 G (9 OZ) *orange marmalade*
2 TABLESPOONS *whisky*
1 TABLESPOON *dijon mustard*
1 *orange*, CUT INTO 6 WEDGES
6 SMALL *rosemary sprigs*
6 *spatchcocks (poussins)*, ABOUT 500 G (1 LB 2 OZ) EACH, RINSED AND PATTED DRY, NECKS TRIMMED
500 ML (17 FL OZ/2 CUPS) *chicken stock*

Preheat the oven to 180°C (350°F/Gas 4).

To make the glaze, combine the marmalade, whisky and mustard in a small saucepan and cook, stirring, over low heat for 5 minutes, or until the marmalade is liquid.

Place a wedge of orange and a sprig of rosemary in the cavity of each spatchcock. Truss with kitchen string and season with sea salt and freshly ground black pepper. Brush two-thirds of the glaze over the spatchcocks, and reserve the remaining glaze.

Transfer the spatchcocks on a rack in a large roasting tin. Pour half of the stock and 125 ml (4 fl oz/½ cup) water into the base of the tin. Roast, covering with foil if they are browning too quickly, for 40–45 minutes, or until the juices run clear when a skewer is inserted into the thickest part of the flesh. Remove from the oven and set aside to rest in a warm place for 10 minutes.

Pour the roasting juices into a small saucepan. Add the remaining stock and the reserved glaze and simmer for 10 minutes, or until reduced and a sauce-like consistency.

Drizzle the spatchcock with the jus and add peas to serve.

Beef wellington *with* béarnaise *sauce*

SERVES *6*
PREPARATION TIME *15 minutes*
COOKING TIME *1 hour, plus cooling and resting time*

1.25 KG (2 LB 12 OZ) *beef eye fillet*, TRIMMED OF SINEW AND EXCESS FAT
1 TABLESPOON *canola oil*
2 TABLESPOONS *brandy*
400 G (14 OZ) BLOCK *ready-made puff pastry*, THAWED
55 G (2 OZ/⅔ CUP) *fresh breadcrumbs*
1 TABLESPOON FINELY CHOPPED *tarragon*
150 G (5 ½ OZ) *duck or chicken liver pâté*
1 *egg*, LIGHTLY BEATEN
1 QUANTITY *béarnaise sauce* (PAGE 95)

Preheat the oven to 210°C (415°F/Gas 6–7). Grease a baking tray.

Tie the meat securely with kitchen string along the length of the fillet, folding the tail end under to make an even cylindrical shape. Grind some black pepper over the beef.

Heat the oil in a large heavy-based frying pan over high heat. Add the beef and brown on all sides, this will take about 10 minutes. Pour in the brandy, light with a match to flambé and cook until the liquid has evaporated. Remove from the heat and set aside until cool enough to handle. Remove the kitchen string.

Lightly flour a work surface and roll out the pastry to form a rectangle about 5 mm (¼ inch) thick that is large enough to encase the beef. Combine the breadcrumbs and tarragon in a small bowl and sprinkle over the pastry. Spread the pâté evenly over the sides of the beef. Place the beef in the centre of the pastry and brush the pastry edges with the egg. Wrap the pastry around the beef, encasing the fillet completely, pressing the edges firmly together. Transfer the pastry-wrapped fillet, seam side down, into a roasting tin. If desired, cut out 1 cm (½ inch) wide strips from the pastry scraps to decorate the surface with a lattice pattern. Brush the pastry with a little more egg. Cut three small slits with the point of a knife across the top of the pastry to allow steam to escape.

Bake for 1 hour for medium (45 minutes for rare and 1½ hours for well done), covering loosely with foil if the pastry is browning too quickly. Rest the beef in a warm place for at least 10 minutes before cutting into thick slices.

Serve with the béarnaise sauce.

Roast goose *with* orange *and* raisin sauce

SERVES *4–6*
PREPARATION TIME *30 minutes*
COOKING TIME *2 hours, plus cooling and resting time*

3 KG (6 LB 12 OZ) *goose*
60 ML (2 FL OZ/¼ CUP) *olive oil*
1 *onion,* ROUGHLY CHOPPED
2 *garlic cloves,* CRUSHED
1 *celery stalk,* FINELY CHOPPED
2 TABLESPOONS ROUGHLY CHOPPED *rosemary*
120 G (4¼ OZ/1½ CUPS) *fresh white breadcrumbs*
FINELY GRATED ZEST OF 1 *orange*
1½ TABLESPOONS *orange juice*
1 *cinnamon stick*
2 TEASPOONS *sea salt*

Orange and raisin sauce

2 *French shallots,* FINELY CHOPPED
125 ML (4 FL OZ/½ CUP) *dry white wine*
125 ML (4 FL OZ/½ CUP) *chicken stock*
250 ML (9 FL OZ/1 CUP) FRESHLY SQUEEZED *orange juice*
40 G (1½ OZ/⅓ CUP) *raisins*

Preheat the oven to 160°C (315°F/Gas 2–3).

Remove any innards from the goose and discard. Rinse the goose inside and out and pat dry with paper towel.

Heat 2 tablespoons of the olive oil in a frying pan over medium heat, add the onion and cook, stirring occasionally, for 3–4 minutes, or until softened. Add the garlic, celery and rosemary and cook, stirring, for 1 minute. Transfer to a large bowl, add the breadcrumbs, orange zest and juice and cinnamon stick, stir to combine, then set aside to cool. Once cool, stuff into the cavity of the goose. Carefully prick the skin all over with a fine skewer and use the skewer to seal the cavity.

Rub the goose with the remaining oil and the sea salt and place, breast side up, on a rack in a large roasting tin. Roast for 1 hour, basting at 20-minute intervals with the juices that have accumulated in the tin. Increase the temperature to 210°C (415°F/Gas 6–7) and roast the goose for a further 40 minutes, or until the juices run clear when the thigh is pierced with a skewer. Remove the goose from the tin and rest in a warm place for 10 minutes.

To make the sauce, pour fat from the roasting tin and reserve for potatoes (p 102). Scrape any drippings from the roasting tin into a saucepan and heat on medium. Add the shallot and cook, stirring occasionally, for 2–3 minutes. Stir in the wine and simmer until reduced by three-quarters. Add the reserved roasting juices and the stock and simmer for 8–10 minutes, or until reduced by half. Pour in the orange juice and cook until syrupy. Reduce the heat, add the raisins and simmer for 1–2 minutes, or until the raisins are softened and swollen. Season with sea salt and freshly ground black pepper. Strain into a serving jug and serve warm with the goose.

Slow-roasted salmon *with* sweet mustard *sauce*

SERVES *6–8*
PREPARATION TIME *10 minutes*
COOKING TIME *1 hour and 30 minutes, plus cooling time*

3.5 KG (7 LB 14 OZ) *whole Tasmanian salmon,* SCALED AND CLEANED
2½ TABLESPOONS *extra virgin olive oil*
lemon slices, TO SERVE

Sweet mustard sauce
90 G (3¼ OZ/⅓ CUP) *dijon mustard*
100 ML (3½ FL OZ) *olive oil*
60 ML (2 FL OZ/¼ CUP) *sherry vinegar*
2 TABLESPOONS *honey*

Preheat the oven to 120°C (235°F/Gas ½). Line a large baking tray with baking paper.

Place the salmon on the prepared tray, season both sides with sea salt and freshly ground black pepper and drizzle on the oil. Cover the salmon with a layer of baking paper and loosely seal the edges. Roast for 1½ hours for medium. To test if the fish is done, pull away the flesh behind the gills; when cooked, the flesh pulls away easily from the bone. Set aside until cool enough to handle.

Meanwhile, to make the sweet mustard sauce, combine the mustard, oil, vinegar and honey in a small saucepan over low heat and simmer for 3 minutes, whisking to emulsify. Season to taste adding more honey, if desired. Allow to cool.

Cut the skin along the back of the salmon from head to tail and gently peel away. Scrape out and discard the grey blood line. Carefully turn over the salmon and transfer to a serving plate, then peel away the skin and blood line from the other side.

Serve the salmon at room temperature with the sweet mustard sauce.

Turkey breast *with* fig, orange *and* cranberry *stuffing*

SERVES *6–8*
PREPARATION TIME *20 minutes*
COOKING TIME *1 hour and 15 minutes, plus resting time*

1.4 KG (3 LB 2 OZ) *de-boned turkey breast*
1 QUANTITY *fig, orange and cranberry stuffing* (PAGE 99)
1 TABLESPOON *olive oil*
125 ML (4 FL OZ/½ CUP) *dry white wine*
500 ML (17 FL OZ/2 CUPS) *chicken stock*
80 G (2¾ OZ/¼ CUP) *redcurrant jelly*
2 TEASPOONS *cornflour (cornstarch)*

Preheat the oven to 180°C (350°F/Gas 4).

Pat the turkey breast dry with paper towel and place, skin side down, on a large chopping board. To butterfly and evenly distribute the breast flesh, slice through the thickest part and open out like a book. Cover with plastic wrap and use a meat mallet to flatten evenly. Spread the stuffing along the centre, leaving a 5 cm (2 inch) outer edge uncovered. Roll up the breast firmly from the short end, tucking in the ends. Tie at regular intervals with kitchen string and skewer the ends if necessary.

Place the turkey, skin side up, in a roasting tin and rub with the olive oil. Pour in the wine and 250 ml (9 fl oz/1 cup) of the stock. Roast for 45 minutes, then pour in the remaining stock and cook for a further 20–25 minutes, or until browned and cooked through. Remove, cover loosely with foil and rest in a warm place for 20 minutes.

Transfer the juices from the tin to a saucepan, add the redcurrant jelly and cook over medium heat, stirring, until the jelly has dissolved. Stir in the cornflour combined with 1 tablespoon cold water and simmer for 2–3 minutes, or until slightly thickened.

Remove the string from the turkey, carve into thick slices and serve with the jus.

Roast venison *with* redcurrant *sauce*

SERVES *4–6*
PREPARATION TIME *10 minutes, plus 2 hours marinating time*
COOKING TIME *30 minutes, plus resting time*

2 TEASPOONS *sea salt*
1 TEASPOON *juniper berries*
2 *rosemary sprigs,* ROUGHLY CHOPPED
650 G (1 LB 7 OZ) *venison eye fillet,* TRIMMED OF SINEW
2 TABLESPOONS *olive oil*
125 ML (4 FL OZ/½ CUP) *red wine*
125 ML (4 FL OZ/½ CUP) *chicken stock*
80 G (2¾ OZ/¼ CUP) *redcurrant jelly*
200 G (7 OZ) *redcurrants* (OPTIONAL)

Combine the salt, juniper berries and rosemary in a mortar and pestle and pound until well crushed.

Place the venison on a large plate and rub with 1 tablespoon of the oil. Roll in the salt mixture until well coated, cover with plastic wrap and place in the refrigerator to marinate for 2 hours.

Preheat the oven to 180°C (350°F/Gas 4).

Heat the remaining oil in a large frying pan over medium–high heat, add the venison and cook on both sides for 2 minutes, or until browned. Transfer to a baking tray and roast for 10–12 minutes for rare. Remove from the oven, cover loosely with foil and set aside to rest in a warm place for 10 minutes before slicing.

Meanwhile, add the red wine to the frying pan and place over medium heat, stirring to scrape up any residue in the base of the pan. Increase the heat and simmer for 2 minutes. Stir in the stock and continue to simmer until reduced by half. Add the redcurrant jelly and whisk for 2 minutes, or until the jelly is melted and combined. Reduce the heat to low and simmer for 10 minutes, or until slightly reduced and syrupy. Strain the redcurrant glaze into a serving jug or bowl.

Slice the venison and serve with the redcurrant glaze and the redcurrants, if desired.

Pan-roasted chicken *with* lentil ragoût *and* Madeira *glaze*

SERVES *6*
PREPARATION TIME *20 minutes*
COOKING TIME *50 minutes, plus resting time*

6 *chicken breasts,* WING BONE ATTACHED AND SKIN INTACT, ABOUT 250 G (9 OZ) EACH
2 TABLESPOONS *olive oil*
375 ML (13 FL OZ/1½ CUPS) *dry Madeira*
375 ML (13 FL OZ/1½ CUPS) *veal stock*
1½ TEASPOONS FINELY CHOPPED *rosemary*

Lentil ragoût

1 TABLESPOON *olive oil*
1 *onion,* FINELY CHOPPED
1 *carrot,* FINELY CHOPPED
1 *garlic clove,* CRUSHED
3 *thyme sprigs*
1 *bay leaf*
200 G (7 OZ/1 CUP) *Puy (tiny blue-green) lentils*
500 ML (17 FL OZ/2 CUPS) *chicken stock*
1½ TABLESPOONS FINELY CHOPPED *flat-leaf (Italian) parsley*

To make the puy lentil ragoût, heat the oil in a saucepan over medium heat, add the onion and carrot and cook, stirring occasionally, for 4 minutes, or until slightly softened. Add the garlic, thyme, bay leaf, lentils and stock, bring to a simmer and cook, stirring occasionally, for 30 minutes, or until the lentils are tender. Mix the parsley into the lentils just before serving.

Preheat the oven to 180°C (350°F/Gas 4).

Meanwhile, heat a large heavy-based frying pan over high heat. Brush the chicken with the oil and season with sea salt and freshly ground black pepper. Cook for 4 minutes, skin side down, turn and cook for 3 minutes. Transfer the chicken to a large roasting tin and roast for 12–15 minutes, or until the chicken is cooked through. Remove the chicken from the tin, cover with foil and allow to rest in a warm place for 5 minutes.

Discard any excess fat from the roasting tin. Add the Madeira, stock and rosemary and simmer over medium heat for 15–20 minutes, or until reduced and syrupy.

Serve the chicken with the Puy lentil ragoût and the rosemary and Madeira glaze.

Tomato *and* herb tartlets

MAKES 6
PREPARATION TIME *25 minutes, plus chilling time*
COOKING TIME *25 minutes*

3 SHEETS *frozen puff pastry*, THAWED
200 G (7 OZ) *ricotta cheese*
50 G (1¾ OZ) FRESHLY GRATED *gruyère cheese*
1½ TABLESPOONS FINELY SNIPPED *chives*
1 TABLESPOON FINELY CHOPPED *flat-leaf (Italian) parsley*
3 x 400 G (14 OZ) TINS *cherry tomatoes*, DRAINED AND RINSED
1 TABLESPOON *olive oil*
4 *anchovy fillets*, FINELY CHOPPED
1 TEASPOON *thyme leaves*
1 LARGE *garlic clove*, CRUSHED
70 G (2½ OZ/2 CUPS) *wild rocket (arugula)*, TO SERVE
2 TABLESPOONS *balsamic vinegar*, TO SERVE

Preheat the oven to 200°C (400°F/Gas 6). Line two baking trays with baking paper.

Cut two 14 cm (5½ inch) rounds from each sheet of pastry, then carefully transfer to the prepared trays. Cut a 1.5 cm (⅝ inch) border on each round using a sharp knife (this allows the pastry to puff around the filling). Place in the refrigerator to chill until ready to use.

Mix the ricotta, gruyère, chives and parsley in a bowl and season with sea salt and freshly ground black pepper. Spread the cheese mixture over the pastry rounds, leaving the border clear — this is very important otherwise the sides of the tarts will collapse.

Place the tomatoes in a bowl, add the olive oil, anchovies, thyme and garlic, season with salt and pepper and toss gently. Arrange the tomatoes on the cheese mixture.

Bake the tarts for 20–25 minutes, or until the pastry is golden. Serve topped with the rocket and drizzled with the balsamic vinegar.

Rack of veal *with* amaretti *and* mustard fruits

SERVES *8*
PREPARATION TIME *20 minutes*
COOKING TIME *1 hour and 15 minutes plus resting time*

80 ML (2½ FL OZ/⅓ CUP) *vegetable oil*
100 G (3½ OZ) *prosciutto,* FINELY DICED
2 *onions,* FINELY CHOPPED
200 G (7 OZ/2 CUPS) GROUND *almonds*
5 *amaretti biscuits (cookies),* CRUSHED
20 G (¾ OZ) *butter,* SOFTENED
2 X *4-rib racks of veal,* ABOUT 1 KG (2 LB 4 OZ)
30 G (1 OZ) *mustard fruits,* FINELY CHOPPED, PLUS 60 ML (2 FL OZ/¼ CUP) *mustard fruit syrup*
2 TEASPOONS *dijon mustard*
60 ML (2 FL OZ/¼ CUP) *amaretto*
80 ML (2½ FL OZ/⅓ CUP) *cream*

Preheat the oven to 200°C (400°F/Gas 6).

Heat half the oil in a frying pan. Add the prosciutto and half the onion and cook, stirring occasionally, for 4 minutes, or until the onion is soft. Place the ground almonds, amaretti and butter in a bowl, add the onion and prosciutto and stir until combined.

To create a cavity for the stuffing, make an incision along the bone of each rack of veal, slightly, but not completely, separating the meat from the bone. Place the prosciutto stuffing in the cavity and tie up the racks with kitchen string, tying in between each bone, as neatly as possible.

Place the veal in a roasting tin and drizzle with the remaining oil. Mix half the mustard fruit with the mustard fruit syrup and brush half of this syrup onto the veal, making sure some of the fruit coats the veal. Roast for 1 hour, basting occasionally with the remaining mustard fruit syrup. Remove the veal from the oven, cover with foil and set aside to rest in a warm place.

Meanwhile, to make the amaretto jus, place the roasting tin over medium heat, add the remaining onion and cook, stirring occasionally, for 5 minutes, or until the onion is soft. Add any extra juices from the veal, the mustard, amaretto and the remaining mustard fruits. Simmer for 2 minutes, or until slightly reduced, then add the cream and simmer for 1 minute. Season to taste.

Slice the veal into individual cutlets and serve drizzled with the amaretto jus and extra mustard fruits if desired.

Spiced loin of pork *with* fig and ginger *compote*

SERVES *6*
PREPARATION TIME *20 minutes*
COOKING TIME *2 hours and 5 minutes, plus resting time*

1 TEASPOON *cumin seeds*
1 TEASPOON *fennel seeds*
1 TEASPOON *coriander seeds*
1 TEASPOON *sea salt*
2 KG (4 LB 8 OZ) *pork loin*
500 ML (17 FL OZ/2 CUPS) *chicken stock*

Fig and ginger compote

1 TABLESPOON *olive oil*
1 *red onion,* FINELY CHOPPED
1 TABLESPOON *fresh ginger,* CUT INTO THIN MATCHSTICKS
125 ML (4 FL OZ/½ CUP) *medium dry sherry,* SUCH AS AMONTILLADO
8 *dried figs,* FINELY DICED
80 G (2¾ OZ/⅓ CUP) *soft brown sugar*
1 TEASPOON GROUND *allspice*
1 TABLESPOON *balsamic vinegar*

Preheat the oven to 220°C (425°F/Gas 7).

Lightly crush the cumin, fennel and coriander seeds and salt using the back of a knife or a mortar and pestle. Rub over the pork.

Place the pork on a rack in a roasting tin and pour the stock into the tin. Bake for 20 minutes. Reduce the temperature to 180°C (350°F/Gas 4) and cook for a further 1¾ hours, or until the juices run clear when a skewer is inserted into the thickest part of the pork. Cover loosely with foil and allow to rest in a warm place for 20 minutes.

Meanwhile, to make the fig and ginger compote, heat the oil in a saucepan. Add the onion and ginger and cook over medium heat for 5 minutes, or until the onion is soft. Pour in the sherry and cook for 5 minutes, or until reduced. Add the figs, sugar, allspice and 125 ml (4 fl oz/½ cup) water and simmer for 15 minutes. Stir in the vinegar and simmer for a further 5 minutes, or until reduced and syrupy.

Slice the pork and serve with the fig and ginger compote.

Merry Christmas
Joyeux Noel
Merry Christmas
Joyeux Noel

Crisp duck confit *with* braised red *cabbage*

SERVES *6*
PREPARATION TIME *30 minutes, plus 7 hours chilling time*
COOKING TIME *3 hours and 30 minutes, plus cooling time*

6 x 250 G (9 OZ) *duck leg quarters*
75 G (2¾ OZ) *rock salt*
1 TABLESPOON *black peppercorns,* LIGHTLY CRUSHED
6 *garlic cloves,* LIGHTLY CRUSHED
5 *star anise*
3 *bay leaves*
1 KG (2 LB 4 OZ) *duck fat*
1 QUANTITY *braised red cabbage* (PAGE 106)

Red wine sauce
1 *French shallot,* THINLY SLICED
375 ML (13 FL OZ/1½ CUPS) *red wine*
60 ML (2 FL OZ/¼ CUP) *port*
3 *garlic cloves,* PEELED AND CUT IN HALF
1 *thyme sprig*
1 LITRE (35 FL OZ/4 CUPS) *veal stock*

Place the duck legs and rock salt in a metal bowl. Add the peppercorns, garlic, star anise and bay leaves. Cover and refrigerate for 6 hours, turning the duck legs occasionally.

Preheat the oven to 100°C (200°F/Gas ½).

Place the duck fat in a large roasting tin and bake for 10 minutes, or until the fat has liquefied. Wipe the salt mixture off the duck legs. Place the duck legs in the duck fat and return to the oven for 2–3 hours, or until the meat is very tender. Allow the duck to cool in the tin. When cooled to room temperature, cover the tin and place in the refrigerator until the fat has solidified.

Meanwhile, to make the red wine sauce, place the shallot, wine, port, garlic and thyme in a small saucepan. Bring to the boil and simmer for 25 minutes, or until reduced and syrupy. Add the stock, bring to the boil and simmer for 50 minutes. Strain into a clean saucepan, push the softened shallot and garlic mixture through a sieve and whisk into the sauce.

Preheat the oven to 180°C (350°F/Gas 4).

Remove the duck legs from the fat, scraping off any excess fat. Heat a non-stick ovenproof frying pan over medium–high heat and fry the duck until browned on all sides. Transfer the pan to the oven and roast for 5–10 minutes, or until the duck is warmed through and the skin is crisp and golden.

Serve with the braised red cabbage and the red wine sauce.

Monkfish *with* lemon butter *and* pickled fennel

SERVES *6*
PREPARATION TIME *6 minutes*
COOKING TIME *10 minutes*

6 *monkfish fillets,* ABOUT 180 G (6¼ OZ) EACH
1 *lemon,* CUT INTO 6 SLICES
60 G (2¼ OZ/¼ CUP) *unsalted butter,* CUT INTO 10 G (¼ OZ) PIECES

Pickled fennel

3 *baby fennel bulbs,* TRIMMED, FRONDS RESERVED AND TORN
60 ML (2 FL OZ/¼ CUP) *Champagne vinegar*
JUICE OF ½ *lemon*
2 TEASPOONS *caster (superfine) sugar*
1 TEASPOON *sea salt*

Lemon butter sauce

150 G (5½ OZ) *unsalted butter*
2 TABLESPOONS *lemon juice*
½ TEASPOON *sea salt*

Preheat the oven to 160°C (315°F/Gas 2–3). Line a roasting tin with baking paper and place the fish fillets on top in a single layer. Top each fillet with a slice of lemon and a piece of butter. Roast for 8–10 minutes, or until the fish is just cooked through.

To make the pickled fennel, thinly slice the fennel using a sharp knife or mandolin and place in a non-metallic bowl with the vinegar, lemon juice, sugar and salt. Add the reserved fennel fronds and stir to combine.

To make the lemon butter sauce, gently melt the butter in a saucepan over low heat for 2 minutes. Remove from the heat and stir in the lemon juice, salt and freshly ground black pepper.

Divide the pickled fennel between six serving plates, top with a piece of fish and drizzle with a little of the lemon butter sauce.

NOTE: If monkfish is unavailable, substitute for rocklobster or ling.

Rolled chicken *with* pistachio *and* truffle *stuffing*

SERVES *6*
PREPARATION TIME *30 minutes*
COOKING TIME *1 hour and 35 minutes, plus cooling and resting time*

20 G (3/4 OZ) *butter*
3 *French shallots,* FINELY CHOPPED
2 TABLESPOONS *brandy*
1 TABLESPOON FINELY CHOPPED *rosemary*
300 G (10 1/2 OZ) MINCED (GROUND) *pork and veal*
50 G (1 3/4 OZ/1/3 CUP) *pistachio nuts,* ROUGHLY CHOPPED
1 *egg,* LIGHTLY BEATEN
10 G (1/4 OZ) *black truffle,* FINELY GRATED
1 TEASPOON *sea salt*
1.9 KG (4 LB 3 OZ) *chicken,* DE-BONED
1 *onion,* ROUGHLY CHOPPED
1 *carrot,* THICKLY SLICED
1/2 *celery stalk,* THICKLY SLICED
1 TABLESPOON *olive oil*
250 ML (9 FL OZ/1 CUP) *white wine*
250 ML (9 FL OZ/1 CUP) *chicken stock*
300 ML (10 1/2 FL OZ) *cream*

Melt the butter in a small frying pan over low heat. Add the shallot and cook, stirring occasionally, for 5 minutes, or until soft. Add the brandy and remove from the heat. Stir in the rosemary and set aside to cool.

Preheat the oven to 200°C (400°F/Gas 6).

Combine the minced pork and veal, pistachio nuts, egg, truffle, salt and cooled shallot mixture in a bowl and, using your hands, mix well.

Place the chicken, skin side down, on a work surface, season with sea salt and freshly ground black pepper. Spread the pork and veal mixture over the chicken. Roll up the chicken from the shortest side – like a Swiss roll (jelly roll) – and tie at intervals with kitchen string.

Scatter the onion, carrot and celery over the base of a roasting tin. Place the chicken on top and drizzle on the oil. Roast for 20 minutes, or until starting to brown. Pour in the wine and stock, reduce the temperature to 180°C (350°F/Gas 4), cover with baking paper and foil and roast for a further 1 hour, or until the juices run clear when the thickest part of the chicken is pierced with a skewer. Transfer the chicken to a platter, cover with foil and rest in a warm place.

Discard the vegetables, place the roasting tin over medium heat and simmer until the liquid is reduced by half. Add the cream and continue to simmer for 5 minutes, or until the sauce has thickened. Taste and season.

Slice the chicken and serve with the cream sauce.

Silverbeet and leek tart *with* cheese *topping*

SERVES *6–8*
PREPARATION TIME *30 minutes, plus 1 hour chilling time*
COOKING TIME *1 hour and 5 minutes, plus cooling time*

Pastry

125 G (4½ OZ/1 CUP) *plain (all-purpose) flour*
75 G (2¾ OZ/½ CUP) *wholemeal (whole-wheat) flour*
125 G (4½ OZ/½ CUP) *unsalted butter,* CHILLED AND CUT INTO CUBES
PINCH OF *salt*
1 *egg yolk*
1 TABLESPOON *iced water*

Filling

500 G (1 LB 2 OZ) *silverbeet (Swiss chard) leaves*
40 G (1½ OZ) *unsalted butter*
3 *leeks,* WHITE PART ONLY, THINLY SLICED
2 TEASPOONS *caraway seeds*
¼ TEASPOON FRESHLY GRATED *nutmeg*
125 G (4½ OZ/½ CUP) *crème fraîche*

Topping

40 G (1½ OZ) *unsalted butter*
40 G (1½ OZ/⅓ CUP) *plain (all-purpose) flour*
250 ML (9 FL OZ/1 CUP) *milk,* WARMED
100 G (3½ OZ) *goat's cheese*
50 G (1¾ OZ/½ CUP) *parmesan cheese,* FINELY GRATED
1 *egg yolk*
2 *egg whites*

Preheat the oven to 180°C (350°F/Gas 4).

To make the pastry, place the flours, butter and salt in the bowl of a food processor and pulse until the mixture resembles fine breadcrumbs. Add the egg yolk and water and process until the mixture just comes together to form a dough. Turn the dough out onto a lightly floured work surface and shape into a disc. Cover with plastic wrap and refrigerate for 30 minutes.

Lightly flour a work surface and roll the dough into a 30 cm (12 inch) circle. Line a 24 cm (9½ inch) loose-based flan (tart) tin with the pastry and trim the edges. Place in the refrigerator for 30 minutes.

Meanwhile, prepare the filling. Plunge the silverbeet into a large saucepan of salted boiling water for 30 seconds. Drain, cool under running water and drain again, squeezing out excess liquid. Finely chop the silverbeet and set aside. Melt the butter in a large frying pan over medium heat. Add the leek and cook for 20 minutes, or until caramelised. Add the silverbeet, caraway seeds and nutmeg and stir well. Set aside to cool. Stir in the crème fraîche.

To make the topping, melt the butter in a saucepan over medium heat. Add the flour and stir for 2 minutes. Gradually add the milk, stirring constantly until smooth, and simmer for 2 minutes, or until slightly thickened. Remove from the heat, stir in the cheeses and egg yolk and continue to mix until melted. Whisk the egg whites in a small bowl until soft peaks form. Gently and quickly fold the egg whites into the mixture.

Spoon the filling into the pastry case and smooth the surface. Spread the cheese topping over the filling to cover the surface. Bake for 35–40 minutes, or until the topping is golden and puffed and the pastry is cooked. Serve warm and top with a handful of watercress to serve.

Roast duck *with* plum *and* ginger glaze

SERVES *4*
PREPARATION TIME *20 minutes*
COOKING TIME *1 hour, plus resting time*

1 TEASPOON *ground ginger*
2 TEASPOONS *ground coriander*
2 TEASPOONS *sea salt*
1 *duck,* ABOUT 2 KG (4 LB 8 OZ)

Plum and ginger glaze
2 TABLESPOONS *soft brown sugar*
15 G (½ OZ) *fresh ginger,* CUT INTO THIN MATCHSTICKS
1 *star anise*
800 G (1 LB 12 OZ) TINS *plums,* DRAINED AND HALVED, SYRUP RESERVED

Preheat the oven to 220°C (425°F/Gas 7).

Combine the ground ginger, ground coriander and salt in a small bowl and rub into the skin and cavity of the duck. Seal the cavity with a metal skewer and tie the legs firmly together with kitchen string.

Place the duck on a rack in a roasting tin and roast for 50–60 minutes. Remove the duck from the roasting tin, cover with foil and allow to rest in a warm place for 15 minutes.

To make the plum and ginger glaze, combine the sugar, ginger, star anise, 375 ml (13 fl oz/1½ cups) of the reserved plum syrup and 80 ml (2½ fl oz/⅓ cup) water in a saucepan and stir over medium heat until the sugar has dissolved. Bring to the boil and simmer for 7 minutes, or until slightly reduced and syrupy. Add the plums and simmer for a further 2 minutes. Serve with the duck.

Pork belly *with* black pudding, apples *and* cider

SERVES *6*
PREPARATION TIME *25 minutes, plus overnight chilling time*
COOKING TIME *3 hours and 50 minutes, plus cooling time*

2 TABLESPOONS *olive oil*
1.5 KG (3 LB 5 OZ) *boneless pork belly*, SCORED
2 TEASPOONS *caraway seeds*
1½ TEASPOONS *sea salt*
250 ML (9 FL OZ/1 CUP) *chicken stock*
20 G (¾ OZ) *butter*
100 G (3½ OZ) *speck*, DICED
3 *green apples*, PEELED AND FINELY DICED
250 ML (9 FL OZ/1 CUP) *apple cider*
2 *black puddings*, CUT INTO 1 CM (½ INCH) THICK SLICES

Preheat the oven to 160°C (315°F/Gas 2–3).

Rub 1 tablespoon of the oil into the pork skin and sprinkle on the caraway seeds and salt. Place the pork on a rack in a roasting tin and pour the stock and 500 ml (17 fl oz/2 cups) water into the base of the tin. Cover with baking paper, then cover with foil. Roast for 3½ hours, or until very tender. Remove from the oven and allow to cool slightly. Transfer to a large plate, cover with baking paper and foil and weight with a heavy baking tray or tins and refrigerate overnight.

When ready to serve, preheat the oven to 220°C (425°F/Gas 7). Cut the pork into six portions, place in a roasting tin and roast for 20 minutes, or until crisp.

Meanwhile, melt the butter in a frying pan. Add the speck and apple and cook, stirring occasionally, for 10 minutes, or until the speck is crisp. Add the cider and cook until the liquid is syrupy.

Heat the remaining oil in a large non-stick frying pan over high heat. Add the black pudding and cook for 2 minutes on each side, or until golden brown.

Place a piece of pork on each serving plate and add a few slices of black pudding on the side. Spoon some of the apple over the top and serve.

Lemon, caper *and* fish *involtini*

SERVES *6*
PREPARATION TIME *20 minutes*
COOKING TIME *30 minutes*

Stuffing

120 G (4¼ OZ/1½ CUPS) *fresh breadcrumbs*
½ TEASPOON CHOPPED *thyme*
1½ TABLESPOONS ROUGHLY CHOPPED *flat-leaf (Italian) parsley*
FINELY GRATED *zest* OF ½ *lemon*
1 TABLESPOON *lemon juice*
½ TABLESPOON FINELY CHOPPED *preserved lemon*
1 TABLESPOON CHOPPED *capers*
DASH OF *worcestershire sauce*
20 G (¾ OZ) *butter,* MELTED

6 X 100 G (3½ OZ) THIN FIRM *white fish fillets,* SUCH AS JOHN DORY OR WHITING, SKIN REMOVED
1 TABLESPOON *vegetable oil*
½ *leek,* WHITE PART ONLY, THINLY SLICED
125 ML (4 FL OZ/½ CUP) *dry white wine*
1 TABLESPOON *lemon juice,* EXTRA
2 TABLESPOONS *cream (whipping)*
2 TABLESPOONS FINELY CHOPPED *flat-leaf (Italian) parsley,* AND *lemon wedges* TO SERVE

Preheat the oven to 180°C (350°F/Gas 4).

To make the stuffing, combine the breadcrumbs, thyme, roughly chopped parsley, lemon zest and juice, preserved lemon, capers, Worcestershire sauce and butter in a large bowl and stir until well combined. Season with sea salt and freshly ground black pepper.

Shape 2 tablespoons of the stuffing into a log roughly the width of the fish fillets. Lay one fillet down on a clean work surface, place the stuffing widthways at one end and roll up the fish to enclose the stuffing. Secure with a toothpick. Repeat with the remaining stuffing and fish fillets.

Heat the oil in a saucepan over medium heat. Add the leek and cook, stirring occasionally, for 4 minutes, or until soft. Pour in the wine, simmer for 1 minute, then add the lemon juice and remove from the heat. Place the fish in a roasting tin, pour the leek mixture over the top and then cover loosely with foil. Roast for 15 minutes, or until the fish is cooked through. Remove the fish and keep warm.

Place the roasting tin over medium heat and simmer until the liquid is reduced by half. Season and add the cream. Reduce for 1 minute, or until slightly thickened.

Serve the fish, remembering to remove the toothpicks, thickly sliced and topped with the cream sauce and the finely chopped parsley. Add lemon wedges to serve.

Herb-crusted rib *of* beef *and* red wine *sauce*

SERVES *6*
PREPARATION TIME *20 minutes*
COOKING TIME *2–2½ hours, plus resting time*

6-bone standing rib beef roast, ABOUT 3.5 KG (7 LB 14 OZ), EXCESS FAT TRIMMED
3 *garlic cloves,* CUT INTO SLIVERS
1 *carrot,* CUT INTO 3 CM (1¼ INCH) PIECES
1 *leek,* WHITE PART ONLY, CUT INTO 3 CM (1¼ INCH) PIECES
1 *onion,* CUT INTO QUARTERS
1 *celery stalk,* CUT INTO 5 CM (2 INCH) LENGTHS
6 *garlic cloves,* PEELED
2 TABLESPOONS *olive oil*
60 G (2¼ OZ/¼ CUP) *dijon mustard*
2 *bay leaves,* TORN
250 ML (9 FL OZ/1 CUP) *red wine*
500 ML (17 FL OZ/2 CUPS) *veal* OR *chicken stock*
green beans WITH *garlic buttercrumbs* AND *hazelnuts,* TO SERVE (PAGE 134)

Herb crust

4 SLICES *bread,* CRUSTS REMOVED, TORN INTO PIECES
2 LARGE HANDFULS *flat-leaf (Italian) parsley leaves*
1 TABLESPOON *thyme leaves*
2 TABLESPOONS *olive oil*

Preheat the oven to 220°C (425°F/Gas 7).

Remove the beef from the refrigerator 30 minutes before cooking. Cut narrow slits in between the rib bones and slide in the garlic slivers.

To make the herb crust, place all the ingredients in the bowl of a food processor and blend until finely chopped and well combined. Set aside.

Scatter the carrot, leek, onion, celery and peeled garlic over the base of a roasting tin and place the beef on top. Drizzle with the oil and season with sea salt and freshly ground black pepper. Roast for 25 minutes, remove from the oven, spread the mustard over the beef, then press the herb crust onto the mustard. Reduce the oven temperature to 180°C (350°F/Gas 4), return the beef to the oven and continue cooking for 1½–2 hours for medium – based on 20 minutes cooking time per 500 g (1 lb 2 oz) of meat. Transfer the beef to a plate, cover with foil and rest in a warm place for at least 20 minutes.

Meanwhile, to prepare the red wine sauce, place the roasting tin over medium heat. Add the bay leaves and wine, scraping any caramelized vegetables from the base of the tin, bring to a simmer and reduce to 80 ml (2½ fl oz/⅓ cup). Pour in the stock and any meat juices that have collected on the plate, bring to a simmer and cook for 10 minutes, or until reduced by half. Strain into a serving jug, cover and keep warm until ready to serve.

Slice the beef into six and serve on warmed plates with yorkshire puddings (page 138), the desired vegetables and the red wine sauce.

Four *cheese* gnocchi

SERVES *4–6*
PREPARATION TIME *45 minutes*
COOKING TIME *40–50 minutes, plus cooling time*

40 G (1½ OZ/¼ CUP) LIGHTLY TOASTED *pine nuts,* TO SERVE
1 SMALL HANDFUL *sage,* TO SERVE
FRESHLY GRATED *nutmeg*

Gnocchi

1 KG (2 LB 4 OZ) *all-purpose potatoes,* SUCH AS DESIREE
300 G (10½ OZ) *plain (all-purpose) flour*
2 LARGE *eggs*
1 TEASPOON *sea salt*
50 G (1¾ OZ/½ CUP) FINELY GRATED *parmesan cheese*

Sauce

115 ML (4 FL OZ/½ CUP) *thick cream*
60 G (2¼ OZ/¼ CUP) *butter*
2 TABLESPOONS *dry white wine*
100 G (3½ OZ) *parmesan cheese,* FINELY GRATED
50 G (1¾ OZ) *gorgonzola cheese,* CRUMBLED
200 G (7 OZ) *mascarpone cheese,* CHOPPED
100 G (3½ OZ/1⅔ CUP) *grated mozzarella cheese*
1 TEASPOON *sea salt*

To make the gnocchi, place the potatoes in a saucepan and cover with cold water. Bring to the boil over medium–high heat and simmer for 20–30 minutes, or until cooked through when tested with a skewer. Drain and set aside to cool. Remove the skin. Push the potatoes through a sieve or grate finely. Combine the potato, flour, eggs, salt and parmesan in a bowl. Tip the dough onto a lightly floured work surface and knead until smooth. Divide into four. Roll each piece of dough into 2.5 cm (1 inch) thick cylinders and, using a flat-bladed knife, cut each cylinder into 2 cm (¾ inch) thick slices. Transfer the slices to a lightly floured tray and refrigerate until needed.

Bring a large saucepan of salted water to the boil. Add one-third of the gnocchi and simmer until they float to the surface. Remove the gnocchi with a slotted spoon and place in a large bowl. Repeat with the remaining gnocchi.

To make the sauce, place the cream and butter in a saucepan and bring to the boil. Reduce the heat to low, add the wine, cheeses and salt and whisk until smooth. Gently stir in the gnocchi to coat with the sauce. Serve immediately, garnished with the pine nuts, sage leaves, and nutmeg.

Mushroom, tarragon *and* taleggio *crumble*

SERVES *6–8*
PREPARATION TIME *15 minutes*
COOKING TIME *25 minutes*

12 G (4½ OZ/½ CUP) *unsalted butter*
4 *French shallots,* FINELY CHOPPED
700 G (24 OZ) *field mushrooms,* TRIMMED AND QUARTERED
2 TABLESPOONS FINELY CHOPPED *tarragon*
6 TABLESPOONS *crème fraîche*
200 G (7 OZ) *taleggio cheese,* RIND REMOVED

Crumble

280 G (10 OZ/3¼ CUPS) FRESH *sourdough breadcrumbs*
2 *garlic cloves,* CRUSHED
180 G (6½ OZ/⅔ CUP) *unsalted butter,* MELTED
50 G (2 OZ/½ CUP) FRESHLY GRATED *parmesan cheese*
50 G (2 OZ/½ CUP) *flaked almonds*

To make the crumble, combine all the ingredients in a bowl, mix well and set aside.

Preheat the oven to 200°C (400°F/Gas 6).

Melt the butter in a large frying pan. Add the shallots and cook, stirring, over medium heat for 2 minutes, or until just soft. Stir in the mushrooms and cook for 5 minutes, or until the mushrooms are slightly wilted. Remove from the heat, stir in the tarragon and crème fraîche and season to taste. Spread the mushrooms in a single layer in two, 1 litre (35 fl oz/4 cup) casserole dishes.

Dot small pieces of the cheese over the mushrooms. Sprinkle the crumble evenly over the top of the two dishes and bake for 20 minutes, or until golden brown and heated through.

FROM TOP LEFT *Pork and sage* stuffing • *Béarnaise* sauce
Bread sauce with *thyme* • *Hazelnut and porcini* stuffing

Pork and sage *stuffing*

MAKES *enough for one chicken or one rolled pork loin*
PREPARATION TIME *10 minutes*
COOKING TIME *15 minutes, plus cooling time*

Melt 20 g (3/4 oz) *butter* in a frying pan, add 1/2 finely chopped small *red onion*, 1/2 finely chopped small *celery stalk* and 2 peeled and crumbled *fat pork sausages.* Cook, stirring occasionally, until lightly browned. Add 1/2 peeled, cored and finely chopped small *green apple* and 20 chopped *sage leaves* and cook until the apple is soft. Season. Transfer to a large bowl and set aside to cool. Add 80 g (2 3/4 oz/1 cup) fresh *sourdough breadcrumbs*, 1/2 teaspoon finely grated *lemon zest* and 1 lightly beaten small *egg* and mix thoroughly. This stuffing is ideal for chicken or pork.

Bread *sauce with* thyme

MAKES *500 g (1 lb 2 oz/2 cups)*
PREPARATION TIME *10 minutes*
COOKING TIME *20 minutes, plus overnight infusing time*

Combine 500 ml (17 fl oz/2 cups) *milk*, 1 peeled and halved with root attached small *onion*, 5 *cloves*, 6 lightly crushed *black peppercorns* and 2 *thyme sprigs* in a saucepan, bring slowly to the boil and remove from the heat. Cool, cover and refrigerate for several hours, or overnight. Strain the milk into a saucepan, discarding the flavourings, and reheat over low heat. Add 80 g (2 3/4 oz/1 cup) fresh *white breadcrumbs* and stir until thickened. Stir in 20 g (3/4 oz) diced *butter*, season well with *sea salt* and a pinch of freshly grated *nutmeg*. Pour into a serving bowl and serve warm.

Béarnaise *sauce*

MAKES *250 g (9 oz/1 cup)*
PREPARATION TIME *5 minutes*
COOKING TIME *15 minutes*

Combine 60 ml (2 fl oz/1/4 cup) *tarragon vinegar*, 80 ml (2 1/2 fl oz/1/3 cup) *white wine*, 2 finely chopped *French shallots* and 2 tablespoons roughly chopped *tarragon* in a small saucepan over medium heat and simmer until reduced to 2 teaspoons. Strain into a bowl, discarding the solids. Place a heatproof bowl over a saucepan of simmering water. Add 3 *egg yolks* and 1 tablespoon *water* and whisk continuously until the mixture has doubled in volume and is pale and creamy. Add 150 g (5 1/2 oz) diced unsalted *butter*, piece by piece, whisking well after each addition until incorporated. Remove from the heat. Stir in the 1 tablespoon finely chopped *tarragon.* Set aside until ready to use.

Hazelnut and porcini *stuffing*

MAKES *enough for one turkey*
PREPARATION TIME *20 minutes, plus 15 minutes soaking time*
COOKING TIME *15 minutes*

Soak 10 g (1/4 oz) dried *porcini mushrooms* in 250 ml (9 fl oz/1 cup) *hot water* for 15 minutes. Drain, reserving the liquid, and chop. Fry 150 g (5 1/2 oz) diced *pancetta* over medium heat until crisp, remove and set aside. Melt 60 g (2 1/4 oz/1/4 cup) *butter* in the pan, add 1 chopped large *onion* and 1 chopped *celery stalk* and cook until soft. Stir in 2 crushed *garlic cloves*, 250 g (9 oz) chopped *Swiss brown mushrooms* and the porcini and cook until soft. Remove from heat and add pancetta, 70 g (2 1/2 oz/1/2 cup) toasted, skinned and chopped *hazelnuts*, 8 slices diced *white bread*, 1/2 teaspoon grated *lemon zest*, 2 tablespoons chopped *flat-leaf (Italian) parsley* and 3 teaspoons chopped *sage leaves*. Moisten with the porcini liquid.

Gravy

MAKES *about 500 ml (17 fl oz/2 cups)*
PREPARATION TIME *10 minutes*
COOKING TIME *25 minutes*

Combine 100 g (3½ oz) chopped *speck*, 1 finely chopped *carrot*, 1 finely chopped *onion* and 8 *sage leaves* in a saucepan and cook, stirring occasionally, over medium heat until golden brown. Add 2 tablespoons *plain (all-purpose) flour* and stir constantly for 2 minutes. Combine 2 tablespoons *red wine*, 500 ml (17 fl oz/2 cups) *chicken stock* and 250 ml (9 fl oz/1 cup) *water* in a jug. Gradually stir the combined liquids into the flour mixture and simmer for 10–15 minutes for a thick gravy. Strain and season to taste. Alternatively, if you have just cooked a piece of meat or poultry, discard all but 2 tablespoons of the pan drippings in the roasting tin and make the gravy following this method.

Cranberry and port *relish*

MAKES *about 280 g (10 oz/1 cup)*
PREPARATION TIME *5 minutes*
COOKING TIME *10 minutes, plus cooling time*

Combine 150 g (5½ oz) fresh or frozen *cranberries*, 80 g (2¾ oz/⅓ cup) *caster (superfine) sugar*, the finely grated zest and juice of 1 *orange*, 1 tablespoon *redcurrant jelly*, 1 teaspoon grated fresh *ginger* and 1 teaspoon *mustard powder* in a small saucepan over medium–low heat and stir until the sugar has dissolved. Cook for a further 5 minutes to soften the cranberries. Mash with a potato masher and continue to cook until thickened and jam-like. Stir in 2 tablespoons *port*, pour into a bowl, cover and refrigerate until needed. Serve slightly warm or at room temperature. Cranberry and port relish will keep, stored in an airtight container, for 1 week in the refrigerator.

Brown rice, currant *and* pistachio nut *stuffing*

MAKES *enough for three medium chickens or one large turkey*
PREPARATION TIME *10 minutes*
COOKING TIME *35 minutes*

Melt 60 g (2¼ oz/¼ cup) *butter* in a saucepan over medium heat. Add 1 finely chopped *onion* and cook, stirring occasionally, until soft. Stir in 1 *cinnamon stick*, 1 teaspoon *fennel seeds*, ½ teaspoon freshly grated *nutmeg* and 200 g (7 oz/1 cup) *long-grain brown rice* and cook for 1 minute. Add ½ teaspoon finely grated *lemon zest*, 125 g (4½ oz) *currants* and 700 ml (24 fl oz) water. Increase the heat to high and bring to the boil, then reduce the heat to low and simmer until the rice is cooked and all the water has been absorbed. Stir in 70 g (2½ oz/½ cup) chopped *pistachio nuts* and 2 tablespoons finely chopped *flat-leaf (Italian) parsley* and season. Set aside to cool. Brown rice, currant and pistachio nut stuffing is delicious with all poultry.

Apple, sage, prune *and* bacon *stuffing*

MAKES *enough for one large turkey*
PREPARATION TIME *10 minutes*
COOKING TIME *10 minutes, plus cooling time*

Melt 30 g (1 oz) *unsalted butter* in a frying pan over medium heat. Add 1 finely chopped large *onion* and cook, stirring occasionally, until soft. Add 200 g (7 oz) diced *bacon* and cook until the bacon is crisp. Remove from the heat and set aside to cool. Place 160 g (5¾ oz/2 cups) fresh *white breadcrumbs*, 2 teaspoons finely chopped *sage*, ½ teaspoon *lemon thyme*, 1 peeled, cored and diced large *granny smith apple*, 125 g (4½ oz) roughly chopped *prunes* and 1 lightly beaten *egg* in a large bowl. Add the bacon mixture, season and stir to combine. Cover and refrigerate until required. Apple, sage, prune and bacon stuffing is ideal for pork, turkey or goose.

FROM TOP LEFT *Gravy* • *Cranberry and port* relish
Brown rice, currant and pistachio nut stuffing • *Apple, sage, prune and bacon* stuffing

FROM TOP LEFT *Horseradish* cream • *Howtowdie style* stuffing
Fig, orange and cranberry stuffing • *Cherry* sauce

Horseradish *cream*

SERVES *8*
PREPARATION TIME *5 minutes, plus 1 hour chilling time*

Place 30 g (1 oz) peeled and finely grated fresh *horseradish* and 500 g (1 lb 2 oz/2 cups) *sour cream* in a bowl, mix to combine and season with *sea salt*. Chill for 1 hour.

Fig, orange *and* cranberry *stuffing*

MAKES *enough for one chicken (double the recipe if roasting a turkey)*
PREPARATION TIME *20 minutes*
COOKING TIME *25 minutes, plus cooling time*

Combine 125 ml (4 fl oz/½ cup) freshly squeezed *orange juice* and 80 g (2¾ oz/⅔ cup) sweetened *dried cranberries* in a small saucepan over medium–high heat. Bring to the boil, reduce heat to low and simmer until the *cranberries* are tender. Set aside. Heat 2 tablespoons *olive oil* in a frying pan, add 1 finely chopped *red onion* and cook, stirring occasionally, over medium heat until light golden. Stir in 1 crushed *garlic clove*, ½ teaspoon *ground cinnamon*, 20 g (¾ oz/½ bunch) chopped *sage* and 2 tablespoons finely chopped *tarragon* and cook for 1 minute. Add 50 g (1¾ oz) *butter*, 80 g (2¾ oz) *dried figs* and the *cranberries* and *orange juice* and cook until the *figs* are tender. Remove from the heat and stir in 160 g (5¾ oz/2 cups) fresh coarse *sourdough breadcrumbs*. Season and set aside to cool. Mix in 1 lightly beaten small *egg* and place the stuffing in the cavity of the bird.

Howtowdie style *stuffing*

MAKES *500 g (1 lb 2 oz/2⅓ cups)*
PREPARATION TIME *15 minutes, plus 2 hours soaking time*
COOKING TIME *15 minutes, plus cooling time*

Soak 2 tablespoons *raisins* in 2 tablespoons *brandy* for 1–2 hours. Heat 1 tablespoon *vegetable oil* in a frying pan, add ½ finely chopped *onion* and a pinch of *sea salt* and cook, stirring occasionally, until the onion is soft. Stir in 100 g (3½ oz) *minced (ground) pork* and 100 g (3½ oz) *minced (ground) chicken* and cook, stirring occasionally, until browned. Add 100 g (3½ oz) cleaned, trimmed and finely chopped *chicken livers* and the *raisins* and *brandy* and cook until slightly reduced. Mix 60 ml (2 fl oz/¼ cup) *cream (whipping)*, 35 g (1¼ oz/¼ cup) chopped salted *pistachio nuts* and 2 teaspoons chopped *sage* and cook until reduced. Add 30 g (1 oz/¼ cup) *oatmeal* and season. Allow to cool.

Cherry *sauce*

MAKES *550 g (1 lb 4 oz/2 cups)*
PREPARATION TIME *10 minutes*
COOKING TIME *40 minutes*

Cut 600 g (1 lb 5 oz) pitted fresh or frozen and thawed *cherries* into quarters. Combine the *cherries*, 2 peeled and coarsely grated *granny smith apples*, 5 finely chopped French *shallots*, 250 ml (9 fl oz/1 cup) *red wine vinegar*, 155 g (5½ oz/⅔ cup) soft *brown sugar*, a large pinch of freshly grated *nutmeg* and 1 *cinnamon stick* in a saucepan and stir over low heat until the *sugar* has dissolved. Bring to the boil, reduce heat to low and simmer, partly covered, for 30–35 minutes, or until syrupy. Serve warm or at room temperature.

Sides

It just isn't Christmas without all the trimmings, so here's a stunning array of accompaniments to share.

Crunchy *roast* potatoes

SERVES *6*
PREPARATION TIME *10 minutes*
COOKING TIME *40–45 minutes*

9 MEDIUM *roasting potatoes,* PEELED AND CUT IN HALF
80 G (2¾ OZ) *goose fat* OR 80 ML (2½ FL OZ/⅓ CUP) *olive oil*

Preheat the oven to 200°C (400°F/Gas 6).

Place the potatoes in a saucepan of lightly salted cold water, cover, bring to the boil and simmer for 5 minutes. Drain and return the potatoes to the pan. Cover with the lid and shake around in the pan in order to roughen the edges.

Melt the fat in a large roasting tin, add the potatoes and baste with the fat. Roast, basting and turning the potatoes once, for 40–45 minutes, or until the potatoes are golden brown. Sprinkle with sea salt and serve.

SB

Maple *syrup* *roasted* parsnips

SERVES *6*
PREPARATION TIME *10 minutes*
COOKING TIME *45 minutes*

700 G (1 LB 9 OZ) *parsnips*, PEELED AND TRIMMED
30 G (1 OZ) *butter*, CHOPPED
1 TABLESPOON *olive oil*
2 TABLESPOONS *pure maple syrup*

Preheat the oven to 200°C (400°F/Gas 6).

Cut the parsnips in quarters lengthways. Heat the butter and oil in a roasting tin, add the parsnips and toss well. Roast for 30 minutes, turning twice. Remove from the oven, drizzle the maple syrup over the parsnips and toss until well coated. Return to the oven to roast for 15 minutes, or until tender and golden.

Braised *red* cabbage

SERVES *6–8*
PREPARATION TIME *10 minutes*
COOKING TIME *45 minutes*

2 TABLESPOONS *olive oil*
500 G (1 LB 2 OZ) *red cabbage,* SLICED
½ *red onion,* THINLY SLICED
2 *garlic cloves,* CRUSHED
1 TEASPOON *sea salt*
1 *granny smith apple,* PEELED AND GRATED
100 ML (3½ FL OZ) *red wine vinegar*
60 G (2¼ OZ/⅓ CUP) *soft brown sugar*
250 ML (9 FL OZ) *dry white wine*
250 ML (9 FL OZ/1 CUP) *chicken stock*

Heat the oil in a deep frying pan over medium heat, add the cabbage, onion, garlic and salt and cook for 2 minutes. Stir in the apple, vinegar and sugar and cook for 3 minutes. Pour in the wine and stock and simmer for 40 minutes, or until the cabbage is tender and the liquid reduced. Serve warm.

Potato *purée*

SERVES *6*
PREPARATION TIME *10 minutes*
COOKING TIME *20 minutes*

1 KG (2 LB 4 OZ) *boiling potatoes,* PEELED AND DICED
200 ML (7 FL OZ) *cream*
75 G ($2^{3}/_{4}$ OZ) *butter,* SOFTENED
1 TEASPOON *sea salt*

Cook the potatoes in a saucepan of boiling salted water for 12–14 minutes, or until tender. Drain, return the potatoes to the pan and cook, stirring, over medium heat for 2 minutes to allow any excess moisture to evaporate. Pass through a mouli or roughly mash and push through a sieve, then return to the pan.

Place the cream and butter in a small saucepan and bring almost to boiling point. Pour onto the potato, add the salt and cook, stirring, over low heat until smooth and warmed through.

Rosemary roasted *pumpkin*

SERVES *6*
PREPARATION TIME *10 minutes*
COOKING TIME *30 minutes*

1.7 KG (3 LB 12 OZ) *pumpkin (winter squash),* SUCH AS *jap* OR *kent*
60 ML (2 FL OZ/¼ CUP) *extra virgin olive oil*
3 TABLESPOONS ROUGHLY CHOPPED *rosemary*

Preheat the oven to 200°C (400°F/Gas 6).

Cut the pumpkin into wedges, remove the seeds, leaving the skin on. Toss in the oil and rosemary and season with sea salt. Place in a roasting tin and cook for 30 minutes, or until golden and tender.

Roasted *balsamic* onions

SERVES *8*
PREPARATION TIME *10 minutes*
COOKING TIME *55 minutes*

- 3 TABLESPOONS ROUGHLY CHOPPED *thyme,* PLUS EXTRA *thyme leaves* TO GARNISH
- 2 TABLESPOONS *balsamic vinegar*
- 1 TABLESPOON *olive oil*
- 1 KG (2 LB 4 OZ) *baby onions,* PEELED

Preheat the oven to 180°C (350°F/Gas 4).

Combine the thyme, vinegar and oil in a large bowl, add the onions and carefully toss to coat. Transfer the onions to a non-stick baking tray and cover with baking paper to prevent the vinegar from burning. Roast for 50–55 minutes, turning once or twice, or until the onions are caramelised and soft.

Mustard *mash*

SERVES *8*
PREPARATION TIME *5 minutes*
COOKING TIME *1 hour, plus cooling time*

2 KG (4 LB 8 OZ) *all-purpose potatoes,* SUCH AS DESIREE, UNPEELED
100 G (3½ OZ) *butter*
3 TABLESPOONS *dijon mustard*
100 ML (3½ FL OZ) *cream*
2 TABLESPOONS *sea salt*

Preheat the oven to 220°C (425°F/Gas 7).

Place the potatoes in a roasting tin and roast for 1 hour, or until very tender when pierced with a small sharp knife. Set aside and allow to cool slightly. When the potatoes are cool enough to handle, peel and place in a large bowl.

Meanwhile, gently heat the butter, mustard and cream in a small saucepan over low heat and stir until melted and combined. Do not boil. Pour over the potato, season with the salt and mash until soft and creamy.

Brussels sprouts *with* chestnuts *and* pancetta

SERVES *6*
PREPARATION TIME *20 minutes*
COOKING TIME *40 minutes, plus cooling time*

600 G (1 LB 5 OZ) *fresh chestnuts,* SCORED, OR 425 G (15 OZ) *tin red chestnuts,* DRAINED, AND RINSED WELL
300 G (10½ OZ) *brussels sprouts*
100 G (3½ OZ) PIECE *pancetta,* FINELY DICED
50 G (1¾ OZ) *unsalted butter*
1 SMALL *red onion,* FINELY CHOPPED
1 TABLESPOON *thyme tips*
1 *garlic clove,* CRUSHED

Preheat the oven to 180°C (350°F/Gas 4).

Place the fresh chestnuts on a large baking tray and toast for 20–25 minutes, or until the shells start to separate. Remove from the oven and wrap in a clean tea towel (dish towel) for 5 minutes, then peel, one at a time, removing the outer and inner skin.

Remove and discard the tough outer leaves from the brussels sprouts. Trim the bases and peel the leaves and continue trimming and peeling until all the leaves have been removed. Set the leaves aside.

Sauté the pancetta in a non-stick frying pan over medium heat for 5 minutes, or until the fat has rendered and the pancetta is crisp. Transfer the pancetta to a plate. Melt half the butter with the rendered fat, add the onion and cook for 5 minutes, or until the onion is soft. Add the chestnuts and toss to warm through. Transfer to a plate and set aside.

Melt the remaining butter in the pan. Add the brussels sprout leaves, thyme and garlic, toss and cook for 1–2 minutes, or until the leaves are tender and bright green. Season with sea salt and freshly ground black pepper. Return the pancetta, onion and chestnuts to the pan and toss gently. Place on a warmed serving dish and serve immediately.

Glazed *baby* carrots

SERVES *6*
PREPARATION TIME *10 minutes*
COOKING TIME *10 minutes*

800 G (1 LB 12 OZ/2 BUNCHES) *baby carrots,* PEELED OR SCRUBBED
60 G (2¼ OZ/¼ CUP) *unsalted butter,* CUT INTO CUBES
1 TEASPOON *caster (superfine) sugar*
FINELY GRATED ZEST OF ½ *lemon*
2 TABLESPOONS *lemon juice*
1 TABLESPOON FINELY CHOPPED *flat-leaf (Italian) parsley* (OPTIONAL)
1 TABLESPOON FINELY CHOPPED *mint* (OPTIONAL)

Place the carrots in a lidded frying pan large enough to hold them in a single layer. Add 60 ml (2 fl oz/¼ cup) water, dot with the butter, sprinkle the sugar over the top and season with sea salt and freshly ground black pepper. Cover with a tight-fitting lid, place over high heat and quickly bring to the boil. Reduce the heat to low, push the lid slightly ajar, and continue to cook until the liquid has evaporated and the carrots are sizzling.

Remove from the heat and shake the pan. Add the lemon zest and juice and the herbs if using and return to the heat for 30 seconds, shaking well. Transfer to a warmed plate and serve immediately.

Braised leeks *with* olive oil, white wine *and* thyme

SERVES *6*
PREPARATION TIME *10 minutes*
COOKING TIME *25 minutes*

3 *leeks* OR 12 *baby leeks,* WHITE PART ONLY
2 TABLESPOONS *olive oil*
1 *garlic clove,* THINLY SLICED
100 ML (3½ FL OZ) *dry white wine*
250 ML (9 FL OZ/1 CUP) *chicken stock*
1 *bay leaf*
3 *lemon thyme sprigs*

Rinse the leeks under running water and drain well. If using larger leeks, cut in half lengthways.

Heat the oil in a non-stick frying pan over medium heat, add the leeks and toss to coat. Stir in the garlic and cook gently for 1 minute, being careful not to brown the vegetables. Pour in the wine, bring to a simmer and cook for 1 minute. Add the stock, bay leaf and thyme, bring to a simmer, cover, and cook for 15–20 minutes, or until the leeks are tender when a knife is inserted in the centre. Season with sea salt and freshly ground black pepper. Transfer to a warmed serving plate and garnish with the bay leaf and thyme sprigs.

Parsnip purée *with* vanilla and *allspice*

SERVES *6*
PREPARATION TIME *10 minutes*
COOKING TIME *25 minutes*

1 KG (2 LB 4 OZ) *parsnips,* PEELED AND CUT INTO 5 CM (2 INCH) PIECES
60 G (2¼ OZ/¼ CUP) *unsalted butter*
¼ TEASPOON *allspice*
¼ TEASPOON *natural vanilla extract*
2 TABLESPOONS *crème fraîche*
60 G (2¼ FL OZ/¼ CUP) *melted butter* (OPTIONAL)
1 TABLESPOON FINELY SNIPPED *chives or* FINELY CHOPPED *flat-leaf (Italian) parsley*

Bring a large saucepan of salted water to the boil. Add the parsnip, return to the boil and simmer for 15–20 minutes, or until the parsnip is tender. Drain well, return to the pan and toss over low–medium heat for 1 minute to allow any excess moisture to evaporate.

Mash the parsnip with the butter, allspice and vanilla and stir over low heat until the butter is melted and well combined. Remove from the heat and stir in the crème fraîche. Drizzle the melted butter over the parsnip purée and sprinkle on the chives or parsley.

Spring onions *and* baby peas

SERVES *6*
PREPARATION TIME *10 minutes*
COOKING TIME *20 minutes*

60 G (2¼ OZ/¼ CUP) *unsalted butter*
12 SMALL *bulb spring onions (scallions),* TRIMMED
1 KG (2 LB 4 OZ) *fresh baby peas,* SHELLED
1 TABLESPOON *caster (superfine) sugar*
4 *mint sprigs*
3 OR 4 LARGE *iceberg lettuce leaves*

Melt the butter in a saucepan over medium heat. Add the spring onions and cook for 2 minutes. Stir in the peas, season with sea salt and freshly ground black pepper and sprinkle on the sugar and mint. Cover with the lettuce leaves and 60 ml (2 fl oz/¼ cup) water, place a tight-fitting lid on the pan and reduce the heat to low–medium. Simmer for 20 minutes, or until the peas are tender. Discard the lettuce and mint and serve immediately.

NOTE: 370 g (13 oz/2 cups) of shelled young fresh broad (fava) beans can be substituted for the peas. Reduce the cooking time to 10 minutes.

Pilaf

SERVES *6*
PREPARATION TIME *5 minutes*
COOKING TIME *35 minutes, plus resting time*

350 G (12 OZ/1¾ CUPS) *long-grain rice*
1 *bay leaf*
3 *black peppercorns*
80 G (2¾ OZ) *unsalted butter,* CUBED
60 G (2¼ OZ/½ CUP) *slivered almonds,* LIGHTLY TOASTED

Preheat the oven to 150°C (300°F/Gas 2).

Rinse the rice under cold running water until the water runs clear, drain.

Bring a large saucepan of salted water to the boil, add the rice and cook for 5 minutes. Drain well. Transfer the rice to a 1.5 litre (52 fl oz/6 cup) casserole dish. Add the bay leaf and peppercorns and dot the butter on top. Cover, seal with foil or a tight-fitting lid and bake for 30 minutes, or until the rice is cooked. Remove from the oven, keep covered and set aside for 10 minutes. Remove the bay leaf and peppercorns. Stir and fluff up the rice with a fork. Sprinkle on the almonds and serve.

TIP: For a variation you can stir in 2 tablespoons of currants, chopped raisins or chopped parsley when fluffing the rice.

Creamed spinach

SERVES *6*
PREPARATION TIME *20 minutes*
COOKING TIME *15 minutes*

1 TABLESPOON *olive oil*
1 SMALL *onion,* VERY THINLY SLICED
2 *garlic cloves,* CRUSHED
500 G (1 LB 2 OZ) *baby English spinach*
50 G (1¾ OZ/½ CUP) FINELY GRATED *parmesan cheese*
FRESHLY GRATED *nutmeg*

White sauce
20 G (¾ OZ) *butter*
1 TABLESPOON *plain (all-purpose) flour*
125 ML (4 FL OZ/½ CUP) *cream*
115 ML (3¾OZ) *thick (heavy) cream*

To make the white sauce, melt the butter in a small saucepan over medium heat, add the flour and stir constantly with a wooden spoon for 1 minute. Add the creams and stir for a further 3 minutes, or until the sauce is smooth and thickened. Set aside.

Heat the oil in a large frying pan over low–medium heat. Add the onion and garlic and cook for 5 minutes, or until soft. Increase the heat to high and add the spinach in four batches, turning gently until wilted. Remove from the heat, add the white sauce and parmesan and stir until combined. Season to taste with sea salt and freshly ground black pepper, sprinkle with the nutmeg and serve with roast beef, lamb or chicken.

Celeriac *and* parmesan *purée*

SERVES *6*
PREPARATION TIME *20 minutes*
COOKING TIME *30 minutes*

2 TABLESPOONS *olive oil*
1 MEDIUM *onion*, VERY THINLY SLICED
1 SMALL *garlic clove*, CRUSHED
2 *small celeriac*, ABOUT 1 KG (2 LB 4 OZ) IN TOTAL, PEELED AND VERY FINELY DICED
125 ML (4 FL OZ/½ CUP) *thick cream*
30 G (1 OZ) *butter*
25 G (1 OZ/¼ CUP) FINELY GRATED *parmesan cheese*
PINCH OF *white pepper*
½ TEASPOON *sea salt*
1 TABLESPOON *truffle oil* (OPTIONAL)

Heat the oil in a saucepan over medium heat, add the onion and cook, stirring occasionally, for 5 minutes, or until soft. Stir in the garlic and celeriac and cook for 7–8 minutes, taking care not to colour the celeriac. Stir in the cream, cover with a sheet of baking paper and a lid and simmer for 15 minutes, or until the celeriac is tender. Add the butter, parmesan, white pepper and salt and stir to combine.

Transfer the celeriac mixture to the bowl of a food processor and process until smooth. Return to the pan and reheat gently. Stir in the truffle oil, if using and serve immediately with lamb or beef.

Hasselback *potatoes*

SERVES *6*
PREPARATION TIME *15 minutes*
COOKING TIME *45 minutes*

- 12 MEDIUM *roasting potatoes,* ABOUT 1 KG (2 LB 4 OZ), PEELED
- 20 G (3/4 OZ) *unsalted butter,* MELTED
- 1 TABLESPOON *olive oil*
- 2 TABLESPOONS *dry breadcrumbs*
- 1 TEASPOON FINELY GRATED *lemon zest*
- 1 SMALL *garlic clove,* CRUSHED
- 1 TABLESPOON FINELY CHOPPED *flat-leaf (Italian) parsley*

Preheat the oven to 180°C (350°F/Gas 4) then line a baking tray with baking paper.

Cut a thin sliver off the base of each potato. Place the potatoes, cut side down, on a chopping board and thinly slice down without cutting all the way through.

Transfer the potatoes to the prepared tray and brush with some of the combined melted butter and oil. Season well with sea salt and freshly ground black pepper. Roast, basting once or twice with the butter and oil, for 35–40 minutes, or until the potatoes are tender when pierced with a skewer.

Meanwhile, combine the breadcrumbs, lemon zest, garlic and parsley in a small bowl and stir in 2 teaspoons of the butter and oil mixture.

Press the breadcrumb mixture evenly over the cooked potatoes and return to the oven for 5 minutes, or until the breadcrumbs are lightly browned. Serve immediately.

Green beans *with* garlic butter crumbs *and* hazelnuts

SERVES *6*
PREPARATION TIME *10 minutes*
COOKING TIME *10 minutes*

15 G (1/2 OZ) *unsalted butter*
1 *garlic clove,* CRUSHED
40 G (1 1/2 OZ/1/2 CUP) *fresh ciabatta breadcrumbs*
FINELY GRATED ZEST OF 1/4 *lemon*
1 TABLESPOON FINELY CHOPPED *flat-leaf (Italian) parsley*
35 G (1 1/4 OZ/1/4 CUP) *hazelnuts,* SKINNED, LIGHTLY TOASTED AND CHOPPED
500 G (1 LB 2 OZ) *green beans,* TRIMMED

Melt the butter in a large frying pan, add the garlic and cook over low heat for 1 minute without browning. Increase the heat to medium–high, stir in the breadcrumbs and lemon zest and toss until the breadcrumbs are lightly browned. Add the parsley and hazelnuts and season with sea salt and freshly ground black pepper.

Meanwhile, bring a saucepan of salted water to the boil, add the beans and cook for 4 minutes, or until tender. Drain well.

Place the beans on a serving dish and pile the garlic butter crumbs on top. Serve at once.

Potato *and* fennel *gratin*

SERVES *8*
PREPARATION TIME *30 minutes*
COOKING TIME *2 hours, plus standing time*

1.5 KG (3 LB 5 OZ) *roasting potatoes,* VERY THINLY SLICED
2 MEDIUM *fennel bulbs,* VERY THINLY SLICED, SOME FRONDS RESERVED
1 LARGE *onion,* FINELY CHOPPED
150 G (5½ OZ/1½ CUPS) FINELY GRATED *parmesan cheese*
450 ML (15¾ FL OZ) *cream*

Preheat the oven to 180°C (350°F/Gas 4). Lightly grease a 2.5 litre (87 fl oz/10 cup) casserole dish.

Place a layer of potato in the prepared dish. Sprinkle over some of the fennel, a little onion and some of the parmesan and season with sea salt and freshly ground black pepper. Continue layering, finishing with a sprinkling of parmesan. Pour on the cream. Cover the dish with a layer of baking paper and a layer of foil. Bake for 1½ hours, uncover and cook for a further 30 minutes, or until the potato is tender and the top is golden. Allow to stand for 10 minutes before serving topped with the reserved fennel fronds.

Yorkshire *puddings*

MAKES *12*
PREPARATION TIME *10 minutes, plus 1½ hour resting time*
COOKING TIME *35 minutes*

200 G (7 OZ) *plain (all-purpose) flour*
½ TEASPOON *baking powder*
PINCH OF *salt*
2 *eggs,* AT ROOM TEMPERATURE
200 ML (7 FL OZ) *milk,* AT ROOM TEMPERATURE
100 ML (3½ FL OZ) *water,* AT ROOM TEMPERATURE

Sift the flour, baking powder and salt into a bowl and make a well in the centre. Add the eggs, milk and water and whisk until the batter is smooth. Set aside to rest for 1½ hours.

Preheat the oven to 180°C (350°F/Gas 4). Liberally oil a 12-hole muffin tin. Place the prepared tin in the oven for 10 minutes. Remove from the oven and quickly pour in the batter to half fill each mould. Immediately return the tin to the oven and bake for 25 minutes, or until the puddings are well risen, golden and crisp.

Sweet potato *and* almond *croquettes*

MAKES *12*
PREPARATION TIME *30 minutes, plus chilling time*
COOKING TIME *1 hour, plus cooling time*

900 G (2 LB) *sweet potato (kumara),* PEELED AND CUT INTO 3 CM (1¼ INCH) DICE
2 TABLESPOONS *olive oil*
½ TEASPOON *ground ginger*
½ TEASPOON *ground cinnamon*
½ TEASPOON *allspice*
½ TEASPOON FRESHLY GRATED *nutmeg*
PINCH OF *sea salt*
1 TABLESPOON *maple syrup*
90 G (3¼ OZ/¾ CUP) *plain (all-purpose) flour*
1 *egg*
1 TABLESPOON *milk*
100 G (5½ OZ/1⅔ CUPS) *flaked almonds,* ROUGHLY CRUSHED
60 ML (2 FL OZ/¼ CUP) *vegetable oil*

Combine the sweet potato, olive oil, spices and salt in a large bowl and gently toss. Place in a shallow baking dish, cover with foil, and roast for 40 minutes, or until golden. Transfer to a large bowl, add the maple syrup and mash with a fork until smooth. Set aside to cool, then refrigerate until completely chilled.

Preheat the oven to 180°C (350°F/Gas 4).

Mould the sweet potato mixture with wet fingers into 12 croquettes about 4 cm (1½ inches) in length and 2 cm (¾ inch) wide.

Place the flour in a bowl. Combine the eggs and milk in a separate bowl and lightly beat. Place the almonds in a third bowl.

Dust each croquette in the flour, then dip in the egg wash and lastly coat with the almonds.

Heat the vegetable oil in a large frying pan over medium heat. Gently fry the croquettes for 1 minute on each side, or until golden. Transfer to a large baking tray and bake for 5–10 minutes to finish cooking.

Danish caramel *potatoes*

SERVES *6*
PREPARATION TIME *10 minutes*
COOKING TIME *25 minutes*

1 KG (2 LB 4 OZ) *new potatoes,* PEELED
80 G (2¾ OZ/⅓ CUP) *caster (superfine) sugar*
20 G (¾ OZ) *unsalted butter*

Place the potatoes in a large saucepan of cold salted water and bring to the boil. Reduce the heat and simmer for 10 minutes, or until just tender (do not overcook). Drain, return the potatoes to the pan and cook for 1–2 minutes to allow excess moisture to evaporate. Remove the potatoes from the heat.

Sprinkle the sugar into a heavy-based saucepan and cook, stirring occasionally, over medium heat until dissolved. Continue to cook for 4 minutes, or until a deep caramel colour. Add the potatoes and toss gently for 4–5 minutes, or until the potatoes have taken on the caramel colour. Add the butter and toss to combine.

Wild mushrooms *and* baby vegetables *blanquette*

SERVES *8*
PREPARATION TIME *20 minutes*
COOKING TIME *55 minutes, plus 30 minutes soaking time*

20 G (3/4 OZ) DRIED *porcini mushrooms*
16 *baby onions,* PEELED
500 ML (17 FL OZ/2 CUPS) *vegetable stock*
800 G (1 LB 12 OZ/2 BUNCHES) *baby carrots,* TRIMMED AND PEELED
350 G (12 OZ/2 BUNCHES) *asparagus,* TRIMMED
300 G (10½ OZ) *pine mushrooms,* CUT INTO CHUNKS
250 G (9 OZ) *Swiss brown mushrooms,* CUT INTO CHUNKS
60 ML (2 FL OZ/1/4 CUP) *lemon juice*
30 G (1 OZ) *unsalted butter*
2 TABLESPOONS FINELY CHOPPED *flat-leaf (Italian) parsley*

Crème fraîche sauce

60 G (2¼ OZ/1/4 CUP) *unsalted butter*
2 TABLESPOONS PLAIN *(all-purpose) flour*
2 *egg yolks*
3 TABLESPOONS *crème fraîche*
30 G (1 OZ) *unsalted butter,* EXTRA, SOFTENED

Soak the porcini mushrooms in 250 ml (9 fl oz/1 cup) warm water for 30 minutes. Drain and squeeze out excess liquid from the mushrooms, reserving the liquid. Roughly chop the mushrooms and set aside.

Meanwhile, cook the onions in salted boiling water for 15 minutes, or until tender when pierced with a knife. Drain and set aside.

Bring the stock to a simmer in a large saucepan, add the carrots and cook for 10 minutes, or until just tender. Remove the carrots with a slotted spoon and set aside. Add the asparagus to the stock and cook for 3 minutes, or until just tender. Remove the asparagus with a slotted spoon and set aside. Transfer the stock and the reserved porcini liquid to a jug.

Place the pine and Swiss brown mushrooms, lemon juice, butter and 60 ml (2 fl oz/1/4 cup) water in a large saucepan over medium–high heat. Cover with a tight-fitting lid and cook for 5 minutes, or until tender. Drain, reserve the cooking juices and set the mushrooms aside.

To make the sauce, melt the butter in a saucepan over low heat. Add the flour and whisk for 5 minutes. Slowly pour in the reserved stock mixture, whisking constantly to make a smooth sauce. Bring to a simmer and stir for 5 minutes, or until the sauce is smooth. Stir in the reserved mushroom juices, season with sea salt and freshly ground black pepper and reduce the heat to low.

To enrich the sauce, whisk the egg yolks and crème fraîche in a small bowl, then stir in the extra butter until combined. Stir in 2 tablespoons of the hot sauce, then stir the egg mixture into the sauce, taking care not to scramble the egg.

Return the carrots, onions, mushrooms, chopped porcini and asparagus to the sauce to heat through. Transfer to a warmed serving dish, sprinkle with the parsley and serve immediately.

Desserts

Round off your yuletide feast with
these impressive and indulgent sweets.

Praline parfait *with* baked baby *apples*

SERVES *10*
PREPARATION TIME *30 minutes, plus 6 hours freezing time*
COOKING TIME *50 minutes*

10 BABY *apples*
50 G (1¾ OZ) UNSALTED *butter*
50 G (1¾ OZ) *soft brown sugar*

Praline

85 G (3 OZ) *hazelnuts*
145 G (5¼ OZ/⅔ CUP) *caster (superfine) sugar*

Parfait

5 *egg whites*
90 G (3¼ OZ) *caster (superfine) sugar*
300 ML (10½ FL OZ) *cream*
½ TEASPOON *natural vanilla extract*

Preheat the oven to 180°C (350°F/Gas 4) then line a baking tray with baking paper.

To make the praline, place the hazelnuts on a baking tray and toast for 8–10 minutes, or until golden. Rub the warm hazelnuts in a clean tea towel (dish towel) to remove the skins. Heat the sugar and 80 ml (2½ fl oz/⅓ cup) water in a small heavy-based saucepan over low heat and stir until the sugar has dissolved. Increase the heat and simmer, without stirring, for 10 minutes, or until dark golden. Working quickly, stir in the hazelnuts and pour onto the prepared tray. Allow the praline to set, then roughly chop and store in a sealed container in the freezer.

To make the parfait, beat the egg whites in a bowl until soft peaks form. Gradually add the sugar and continue to beat until the mixture is glossy and firm peaks form. Beat the cream and vanilla in a separate bowl using electric beaters until soft peaks form. Fold the cream into the egg whites, one-third at a time, until just combined. Add the chopped praline and pour into a 24 x 7.5 cm (9½ x 3 inch) terrine tin greased and lined with plastic wrap. Freeze for 6 hours, or until set.

Preheat the oven to 160°C (315°F/Gas 2–3).

Place the apples on a large baking tray, dot the top of each apple with 1 teaspoon of the butter and sprinkle each with 1 teaspoon of the brown sugar. Bake for 25 minutes, or until the apples are soft.

Remove the praline parfait from the tin, discard the plastic wrap and cut into 10 slices. Serve slices of the parfait with a baked baby apple.

Raspberry *and* pink Champagne jelly *with* rosewater sorbet

SERVES *8*
PREPARATION TIME *40 minutes, plus overnight freezing time and 4 hours chilling time*
COOKING TIME *5 minutes, plus cooling time*

220 G (7¾ OZ) *raspberries*
700 ML (24 FL OZ) *pink Champagne* OR *sparkling wine*
230 G (8¼ OZ/1 CUP) *caster (superfine) sugar*
3 TEASPOONS *powdered gelatine* SOFTENED IN 2½ TABLESPOONS *pink Champagne* OR *sparkling wine.*

Rosewater sorbet

200 ML (7 FL OZ) *orange juice*
2½ TABLESPOONS *lemon juice*
250 G (9 OZ) *caster (superfine) sugar*
100 ML (3½ FL OZ) *glucose syrup*
3 TEASPOONS *rosewater*
200 G (7 OZ) *plain yoghurt*

To make the rosewater sorbet, place the orange and lemon juice, sugar and glucose syrup in a saucepan over low heat and stir until the sugar and syrup have dissolved. Remove from the heat and add the rosewater. Pour into a bowl, set on top of another bowl filled with ice and allow the mixture to cool. Fold in the yoghurt and churn in an ice-cream machine according to the manufacturer's instructions. Spoon into a container, cover and freeze overnight.

Place 60 g (2¼ oz/½ cup) of the raspberries in a saucepan and crush with a fork, add the Champagne or sparkling wine and sugar and stir over low heat until the sugar has dissolved. Bring to the boil and simmer for 1 minute, add the gelatine mixture and whisk to combine. Strain, discarding the solids, and set aside to cool to room temperature.

Place eight glasses on a tray. Divide the remaining raspberries among the glasses and pour in the jelly. Refrigerate for 4 hours, or until set.

Top each jelly with a scoop of rosewater sorbet and serve.

Blackberry semifreddo *with* orange caramel

SERVES *8–10*
PREPARATION TIME *20 minutes, plus 6 hours freezing time*
COOKING TIME *15 minutes, plus cooling time*

300 G (10½ OZ/2⅓ CUPS) *blackberries*
3 *eggs*
3 *egg yolks*
1 TEASPOON *natural vanilla extract*
230 G (8¼ OZ/1 CUP) *caster (superfine) sugar*
375 ML (13 FL OZ/1½ CUPS) *cream*, FOR WHIPPING

Orange caramel

250 G (9 OZ) *soft brown sugar*
125 ML (4 FL OZ/½ CUP) FRESHLY SQUEEZED *orange juice*

To make the blackberry semifreddo, purée the blackberries and set aside. Combine the eggs, egg yolks, vanilla and sugar in a large heatproof bowl and place over a saucepan of simmering water. Beat using electric beaters for 5 minutes, or until heated through and frothy. Remove the bowl from the heat and beat for a further 5 minutes, or until the mixture has cooled. Beat the cream in a separate bowl until soft peaks form. Fold the egg mixture into the cream, one-third at a time, until just combined. Fold in the blackberry purée until smooth and pour into a 10 x 20 cm (4 x 8 inch) deep loaf (bar) tin. Cover with foil and freeze for 4–6 hours, or until set

To make the orange caramel, place the sugar and half the orange juice in a small heavy-based saucepan over medium heat and stir to dissolve the sugar. Increase the heat and boil until the temperature reaches 135°C (280°F) on a sugar (candy) thermometer. Remove from the heat and add the remaining orange juice. Set aside to cool, then strain.

Serve scoops of the semifreddo drizzled with the orange caramel.

Apricot crumble *tart*

SERVES *6–8*
PREPARATION TIME *45 minutes*
COOKING TIME *1 hour and 15 minutes, plus cooling time*

icing (confectioners') sugar, FOR DUSTING
vanilla bean ice-cream, TO SERVE

Pastry

185 G (6½ OZ/1½ CUPS) *plain (all-purpose) flour*
3 TABLESPOONS *icing (confectioners') sugar*
115 G (4 OZ) *unsalted butter*, CHILLED AND CUT INTO CUBES
2 LARGE *egg yolks*
2–3 TEASPOONS *iced water*

Apricot filling

500 G (1 LB 2 OZ) *dried apricots*, SLICED
55 G (2 OZ/¼ CUP) *caster (superfine) sugar*
1 *vanilla bean*, SPLIT LENGTHWAYS AND SEEDS SCRAPED
1 *cinnamon stick*
1 TEASPOON FINELY GRATED *orange zest*
1 TEASPOON FINELY GRATED *lemon zest*
1 TABLESPOON *lemon juice*
1 TABLESPOON *custard powder*

Crumble topping

40 G (1½ OZ/¼ CUP) *macadamia nuts*
100 G (3½ OZ) *plain (all-purpose) flour*
55 G (2 OZ/¼ CUP) *caster (superfine) sugar*
40 G (1½ OZ) *ground almonds*
75 G (2¾ OZ) *unsalted butter*, SOFTENED

To make the pastry, sift the flour, sugar and a pinch of salt into a large bowl. Make a well in the centre, add the butter and egg yolks and work into the flour with your fingertips. Add iced water if necessary, and form a ball. Flatten slightly, cover with plastic wrap. Refrigerate for 30 minutes.

Preheat the oven to 170°C (325°F/Gas 3). Grease a loose-based, fluted rectangular 12 x 34 cm (5 x 8½ inch) flan (tart) tin. Roll out the pastry on a lightly floured work surface until 3 mm (⅛ inch) thick. Gently press the pastry into the prepared tin using your fingertips. Trim away any excess pastry, prick the base with a fork and refrigerate for 15 minutes. Line the base with baking paper, pour in some uncooked rice and bake for 10 minutes. Remove the paper and rice and bake for 5 minutes, or until just golden. Set aside to cool.

To make the apricot filling, place the apricots, sugar, vanilla bean and seeds, cinnamon stick, zests, lemon juice and 500 ml (17 fl oz/2 cups) water in a small saucepan. Cover, place over medium heat and bring to the boil. Reduce the heat to low and simmer for 20–25 minutes, or until soft. Mix the custard powder and 1–2 tablespoons water in a small bowl until smooth. Stir into the fruit mixture and cook over low–medium heat for 5 minutes, or until thickened. Remove from the heat, discard the vanilla bean and cinnamon stick and set aside to cool.

Increase the oven temperature to 180°C (350°F/Gas 4). To make the crumble, chop macadamias and combine in a bowl with flour, sugar, ground almonds. Rub in the butter until crumbly.

Spoon the apricot filling into the pastry case. Sprinkle the crumble evenly over the top and bake for 25–30 minutes, or until golden. Dust lightly with the icing sugar and serve warm with a scoop of the ice cream.

Cardamom, chocolate *and* pear *trifle*

SERVES *8–10*
PREPARATION TIME *1 hour and 20 minutes, plus overnight chilling time*
COOKING TIME *1 hour, plus cooling time*

115 ML (3¾ FL OZ) *port*
45 G (1¾ OZ/½ CUP) *flaked almonds,* LIGHTLY TOASTED
25 X 30 CM (10 X 12 INCH) *ready-made sponge cake*

Cardamom cream
250 ML (9 FL OZ/1 CUP) *milk*
55 G (2 OZ/¼ CUP) *caster (superfine) sugar*
2 *egg yolks*
1 TEASPOON *natural vanilla extract*
2 TABLESPOONS *cornflour (cornstarch)*
500 ML (17 FL OZ/2 CUPS) *cream,* FOR WHIPPING
½ TEASPOON *ground cardamom*

Pears
500 G (1 LB 2 OZ) *sugar*
2½ TABLESPOONS *lemon juice*
1 TABLESPOON *natural vanilla extract*
100 ML (3½ FL OZ) *port*
6 *packham pears,* PEELED AND CORED

Chocolate sauce
250 ML (9 FL OZ/1 CUP) *cream*
115 G (4 OZ) *dark chocolate,* ROUGHLY CHOPPED
20 G (¾ OZ) *butter,* CUT INTO CUBES

To make the cardamom cream, combine 185 ml (6 fl oz/¾ cup) of the milk and half the sugar in a saucepan over medium heat and bring to simmering point. Remove from the heat and set aside. Beat the egg yolks, vanilla and cornflour with the remaining milk and sugar in a bowl using electric beaters until well combined. Gradually whisk in the hot milk mixture. Return the mixture to the cleaned saucepan and cook, whisking constantly, over medium heat until thickened. Allow to cool for 10 minutes. Transfer to a bowl, press plastic wrap over the top to seal and refrigerate until chilled. Place the cream and cardamom in a separate bowl and beat until firm peaks form. Remove the custard from the refrigerator, whisk well, then fold in the cream mixture. Cover and return to the refrigerator.

To make the pears, place the sugar, lemon juice, vanilla, port and 500 ml (17 fl oz/2 cups) water in a saucepan. Bring to the boil, stirring until the sugar has dissolved. Remove from the heat. Slice each pear into quarters, then cut each quarter in half lengthways. Place the pear in the syrup and press a piece of baking paper on top, to keep the pear pieces submerged. Simmer over low–medium heat for 20–25 minutes, or until tender. Remove from the heat and allow the pear to cool in the syrup.

To make the chocolate sauce, place the cream in a small saucepan and bring just to the boil. Place the chocolate in a bowl, pour on the cream and whisk in the butter until smooth. Set aside to cool to room temperature.

To assemble the trifle, cut the sponge cake into 2 cm (¾ inch) squares. Mix 500 ml (17 fl oz/2 cups) of the pear poaching syrup with the port. Place the sponge in a large bowl, drizzle on the syrup and port mixture and toss gently. Place one-third of the sponge in the base of a large glass bowl and top with one-third of the pear slices, one-third of the chocolate sauce and one-third of the cardamom cream. Repeat with the remaining ingredients, finishing with a layer of the cardamom cream. Scatter on the almonds, cover and refrigerate overnight, if possible.

Christmas strudel *with* eggnog *sauce*

SERVES *8*
PREPARATION TIME *40 minutes, plus 10 minutes soaking time*
COOKING TIME *1 hour*

185 G (6½ OZ/1 CUP) *figs,* DRIED, ROUGHLY CHOPPED
180 G (6¼ OZ/1 CUP) *dried apricots,* HALVED
2 TABLESPOONS *Marsala* OR *rich sherry*
60 G (2¼ OZ/½ CUP) *raisins*
60 G (2¼ OZ/½ CUP) *walnut pieces,*
1 *green apple,* PEELED, CORED AND CHOPPED
FINELY GRATED *zest* OF 1 *orange*
½ TEASPOON *ground cinnamon*
½ TEASPOON *allspice*
60 G (2¼ OZ/½ CUP) *walnut pieces,* ROUGHLY CHOPPED
40 G (1½ OZ/½ CUP) *fresh breadcrumbs*
6 SHEETS *filo pastry*
90 G (3¼ OZ/⅓ CUP) *butter,* MELTED
icing (confectioners') sugar, FOR DUSTING

Eggnog sauce

2 *eggs*
55 G (2 OZ/¼ CUP) *soft brown sugar*
1 TEASPOON *natural vanilla extract*
1 TEASPOON *cornflour (cornstarch)*
½ TEASPOON FINELY GRATED *lemon zest*
185 ML (6 FL OZ/¾ CUP) *cream*
125 ML (4 FL OZ/½ CUP) *milk*
60 ML (2 FL OZ/¼ CUP) *whisky, rum or brandy*

To make the eggnog sauce, whisk the eggs, sugar, vanilla, cornflour and lemon zest in a saucepan until well combined. Add the cream and milk and stir constantly over low heat until thickened – do not allow to boil. Cool a little then stir in the liquor. Pour into a serving jug or bowl, cover and refrigerate until ready to serve. Serve either slightly warmed or at room temperature.

Preheat the oven to 180°C (350°F/Gas 4). Grease a large baking tray.

Combine the figs and apricots in a small saucepan and add water to cover. Bring slowly to the boil, remove from the heat and set aside for 10 minutes to soften. Drain, transfer to a bowl and sprinkle over the Marsala or sherry. Stir in the raisins, walnut pieces, apple, orange zest and spices.

Mix the chopped walnut pieces and the breadcrumbs in a small bowl.

Place one sheet of the filo pastry on the baking tray, brush with some of the melted butter and scatter on one-fifth of the walnut and breadcrumb mixture. Repeat the layering of the pastry and the walnut mixture four times more, finishing with a sheet of buttered pastry. Spoon the fig mixture along one long edge of the pastry, leaving a 3 cm (1¼ inch) border at the short ends. Fold in the short ends and firmly roll up the pastry to enclose the filling. Place the strudel, seam side down, on the tray and brush with the remaining butter. Bake for 30–35 minutes, or until crisp and golden brown. Sprinkle liberally with the icing sugar while hot. Cut, at an angle, into eight thick slices and serve warm with the eggnog sauce.

Cranberry *creams*

SERVES *6*
PREPARATION TIME *20 minutes, plus 4 hours chilling time*
COOKING TIME *30 minutes*

4 *egg yolks*
55 G (2 OZ/¼ CUP) *caster (superfine) sugar*
300 ML (10½ FL OZ) *cream (whipping)*
125 ML (4 FL OZ/½ CUP) *milk*
FINELY GRATED *zest* OF 1 *orange*
icing (confectioners') sugar, TO SERVE

Cranberry compote

150 G (5½ OZ) FRESH OR FROZEN *cranberries*
55 G (2 OZ/¼ CUP) *caster (superfine) sugar*
JUICE OF 1 *orange*

Preheat the oven to 150°C (300°F/Gas 2). Place six 170 ml (5½ fl oz/⅔ cup) ceramic pots or decorative cups in a large baking tin.

To make the cranberry compote, combine the cranberries, sugar and orange juice in a small saucepan. Bring to the boil and stir until the sugar has dissolved. Reduce the heat to low, mash the cranberries with a potato masher and cook for 5 minutes, or until thick. Spoon the cranberry compote evenly over the base of each pot.

Beat the egg yolks and caster sugar in a bowl using electric beaters until thick and creamy. Combine the cream, milk and orange zest in a saucepan and bring to scalding point. Gradually beat the cream mixture into the egg yolk mixture. Return the mixture to the cleaned saucepan and stir constantly over low heat for 2–3 minutes, or until the mixture has thickened a little and coats the back of the spoon.

Pour the custard over the back of the spoon into the pots, so as not to disturb the fruit. Half fill the baking tin with boiling water and bake for 20 minutes, or until the custard is just set. Take care not to overcook, the centre should wobble slightly. Set aside to cool, cover with plastic wrap and refrigerate for 4 hours, or overnight.

To serve, sift the icing sugar over each pot of cranberry cream.

Nougat and pistachio semifreddo *with* raspberry *sauce*

SERVES *8–10*
PREPARATION TIME *30 minutes, plus overnight freezing time*
COOKING TIME *5 minutes*

3 *eggs,* SEPARATED
115 G (4 OZ/½ CUP) *caster (superfine) sugar*
1 TEASPOON *natural vanilla extract*
100 G (3½ OZ) *soft nougat,* CHOPPED INTO SMALL PIECES
50 G (1¾ OZ/⅓ CUP) *pistachio nuts,* TOASTED AND CHOPPED
40 G (1½ OZ/⅓ CUP) *sweetened dried cranberries,* CHOPPED
300 ML (10½ FL OZ) *thickened cream*

Raspberry sauce

200 G (7 OZ) FRESH OR FROZEN *raspberries*
55 G (2 OZ/¼ CUP) *caster (superfine) sugar*
1 TABLESPOON *liqueur,* SUCH AS *Grand Marnier or kirsch* (OPTIONAL)

Line the base and sides of a 10 x 20 cm (4 x 8 inch) deep loaf (bar) tin or 23 cm (9 inch) springform tin with plastic wrap, allowing the plastic to overhang the sides.

Beat the egg yolks, sugar and vanilla in a bowl using electric beaters until thick and creamy. Then gently fold in the nougat, the pistachio nuts and the cranberries.

Lightly whip the cream in a large bowl using electric beaters. Beat the egg whites in a separate bowl using clean beaters until soft peaks form. Quickly and gently fold the cream, and then the egg white through the nougat mixture.

Carefully spoon the mixture into the prepared tin and smooth the surface with the back of a spoon. Cover with the overhanging plastic wrap and freeze overnight.

Meanwhile, make the raspberry sauce. Place the raspberries and sugar in a saucepan and gently stir, leaving the berries whole, over low heat for 2–3 minutes, or until the juices run. Remove from the heat, cool to room temperature and stir in the liqueur, if using.

To serve, invert the semifreddo onto a plate and remove the plastic, cut into thick slices and spoon on the raspberry sauce.

NOTE: Spray the loaf tin with a little oil before lining with plastic wrap so that the plastic sticks on firmly and smoothly. The nougat can contain fruit and/or nuts and be any flavour you desire.

Quince ice cream terrine *with* sticky quince

SERVES *8–10*
PREPARATION TIME *20 minutes, plus 8 hours freezing time*
COOKING TIME *1 hour and 45 minutes*

100 ML (3½ FL OZ) *brandy*
220 G (7¾ OZ) *caster (superfine) sugar*
1 *cinnamon stick*
1 STRIP *lemon peel*
2 SMALL *quinces*, PEELED, QUARTERED AND CORED
4 *egg yolks*
300 ML (10½ FL OZ) *thickened cream*, LIGHTLY WHIPPED
¼ TEASPOON FRESHLY GRATED *nutmeg*

Combine the brandy, sugar, cinnamon, lemon peel and 1 litre (35 fl oz/ 4 cups) water in a saucepan over high heat and, stirring to dissolve the sugar, bring to the boil. Cut each quince quarter into three wedges and add to the syrup. Reduce the heat to low and cook for 45 minutes, or until the quince is tender and a pale apricot colour. Remove the quince with a slotted spoon and set aside.

Measure the quince poaching syrup and add half the quantity to the quince. Return the remaining syrup to the pan and cook over medium heat until reduced and the temperature reaches 110°C (225°F) on a sugar (candy) thermometer. Remove from the heat.

Place the egg yolks in a large bowl and, while beating with electric beaters, slowly pour in the hot syrup in a thin steady stream. Continue beating until the mixture is pale and doubled in volume. Fold in the cream and nutmeg and spoon into a 1 litre 10 x 15 cm (35 fl oz/4 cup) (4 x 6 inches) terrine tin. Cover with plastic wrap and freeze for 8 hours.

Meanwhile, place the quince and syrup in a saucepan over low–medium heat and cook for 45 minutes, or until the quince is a deep red colour and the syrup has reduced by half, adding a little extra water if necessary to prevent the quince from burning. Set aside to cool.

When ready to serve, wrap hot damp tea towels (dish towels) around the outside of the terrine tin to loosen the ice cream. Invert the ice cream onto a serving plate and decorate with the poached quince. Cut into even slices and drizzle on the syrup.

Cherry *pavlova*

SERVES *8–10*
PREPARATION TIME *25 minutes*
COOKING TIME *1 hour and 30 minutes, plus 1 hour cooling time*

6 *egg whites*, AT ROOM TEMPERATURE
345 G (12 OZ/1½ CUPS) *caster (superfine) sugar*
2 TEASPOONS *cornflour (cornstarch)*
1 TEASPOON *white vinegar*

Cherry syrup

2 TABLESPOONS *soft brown sugar*
90 ML (3 FL OZ) *brandy*
90 ML (3 FL OZ) *red wine*
750 G (1 LB 10 OZ) *cherries*, PITTED

Mascarpone cream

250 G (9 OZ) *mascarpone cheese*
300 ML (10½ FL OZ) *cream*, LIGHTLY WHIPPED

Preheat the oven to 120°C (235°F/Gas ½). Line a baking tray with baking paper and draw a 24 cm (9½ inch) circle on the paper.

Beat the egg whites in a large bowl with electric beaters until soft peaks form. Gradually add the sugar, 1 tablespoon at a time, and beat until the mixture is smooth, thick and glossy. Fold in the cornflour and vinegar.

Spoon the pavlova mixture onto the prepared tray, keeping within the circle and building up the pavlova to form a mound. Bake for 1½ hours, or until crisp on the outside. Turn off the oven and, with the door slightly ajar, allow the pavlova to cool for 1 hour.

Meanwhile, to make the cherry syrup, place the sugar, brandy and wine in a saucepan over medium heat and stir until the sugar has dissolved. Bring to the boil, reduce the heat to low and add the cherries. Simmer for 5 minutes, then remove the cherries with a slotted spoon and place in a large heatproof bowl. Continue to simmer the syrup for 10–15 minutes, or until the liquid has reduced by half. Pour the syrup over the cherries and set aside to cool.

To make the mascarpone cream, combine the mascarpone and cream in a bowl.

Carefully spread the mascarpone cream over the top of the cooled pavlova. Top with the cherries and syrup and serve immediately.

Rhubarb parfait *with* honey wafers

SERVES *8*
PREPARATION TIME *30 minutes, plus overnight freezing time*
COOKING TIME *20 minutes*

700 G (1 LB 9 OZ) *rhubarb,* CUT INTO 2 CM (3/4 INCH) LENGTHS
250 G (9 OZ) *caster (superfine) sugar*
2 *eggs*
2 *egg yolks*
1 TEASPOON *vanilla bean paste*
300 ML (10 1/2 FL OZ) *cream,* LIGHTLY WHIPPED

Honey wafers

30 G (1 OZ) *butter,* SOFTENED
3 TABLESPOONS *honey*
1 *egg white*
40 G (1 1/2 OZ/1/3 CUP) *plain (all-purpose) flour*

Combine the rhubarb, 170 g (6 oz/3/4 cup) of the sugar and 2 tablespoons water in a saucepan. Bring to the boil and simmer, covered, for 3 minutes, or until the rhubarb is just soft. Allow to cool without stirring.

Grease a 10 x 20 cm (4 x 8 inch) loaf (bar) tin and line with plastic wrap, allowing the plastic wrap to overhang the long sides.

Combine the eggs, egg yolks, vanilla bean paste and the remaining sugar in a heatproof bowl. Place over a saucepan of simmering water and beat with electric beaters until the sugar has dissolved and the mixture is warm. Remove from the heat and continue to beat for 3 minutes, or until cool, light and fluffy. Gently fold in half of the rhubarb mixture, then fold in the cream.

Pour the parfait mixture into the prepared tin, cover with the overhanging plastic wrap and freeze overnight, or until firm.

Preheat the oven to 180°C (350°F/Gas 4). Line a baking tray with baking paper and draw six 4 x 18 cm (1 1/2 x 14 inch) rectangles on the paper.

To make the honey wafers, beat the butter, honey, egg white and flour in a small bowl using electric beaters for 30 seconds. Scrape down the side of the bowl and beat for a further 30 seconds, or until the mixture is light in colour.

Spread a thin layer of the tuile mixture, keeping within the rectangles, on the baking paper. Bake for 4 minutes, or until golden brown. Working quickly, run a spatula under a tuile, wrap it around a wooden rolling pin in a spiral pattern and hold in place until cool enough to keep its shape. Repeat with the remaining mixture.

Remove the parfait from the tin, discarding the plastic wrap, and cut into eight slices. Serve with a honey tuile and a spoonful of the remaining poached rhubarb.

NOEL

Iced almond *and* muscatel *puddings*

SERVES *8–12*
PREPARATION TIME *20 minutes, plus overnight soaking and freezing time*
COOKING TIME *15 minutes*

- 50 G (1¾ OZ/⅓ CUP) TOASTED BLANCHED *almonds,* ROUGHLY CHOPPED
- 80 G (2¾ OZ) DRIED *muscatels*
- 1 TEASPOON *mixed (pumpkin pie) spice*
- ½ TEASPOON *ground cinnamon*
- 30 ML (1 FL OZ) *amaretto or rum*
- 200 G (7 OZ) *caster (superfine) sugar*
- 8 *egg yolks*
- 600 ML (21 FL OZ) *thick cream,* WHIPPED TO SOFT PEAKS
- 6 *amaretti biscuits (cookies),* CRUMBLED
- 250 G (9 OZ) *dark chocolate,* MELTED

Combine the almonds, muscatels, spices and amaretto or rum in a small bowl, cover and soak overnight.

Place the sugar and 200 ml (7 fl oz) water in a small heavy-based saucepan over low heat and stir to dissolve the sugar. Increase the heat and bring to the boil. Continue cooking until the temperature reaches 110°C (230°F) on a sugar (candy) thermometer. Remove from the heat.

Place the egg yolks in a large bowl and whisk, using electric beaters, while slowly pouring in the hot syrup in a thin steady stream. Continue whisking until the mixture is pale, doubled in volume and cool. Fold in the cream, then fold in the fruit mixture and finally fold in the amaretti.

Spoon into eight 200 ml (7 fl oz) or twelve 125 ml (4 fl oz/½ cup) individual ramekins or dariole moulds, cover with plastic wrap and freeze overnight. To unmould, wrap a hot damp cloth around the moulds and invert onto a tray lined with baking paper. Return to the freezer until ready to serve.

Spoon the melted chocolate over the top of each ice-cream pudding, allowing it to drizzle down the sides. Return to the freezer for a few minutes to set, place on serving plates and serve.

Blood orange panna cotta *with* orange blossom *syrup*

SERVES *8*
PREPARATION TIME *20 minutes, plus 4 hours chilling time*
COOKING TIME *20 minutes, plus cooling time*

3 *blood oranges,* SEGMENTED
chopped pistachio nuts, TO SERVE
orange slices, TO SERVE

Panna cotta

3 *gelatine leaves*
1 LITRE (35 FL OZ/4 CUPS) *thick cream*
145 G (5¼ OZ/⅔ CUP) *caster (superfine) sugar*
FINELY GRATED *zest* OF 2 *blood oranges*

Syrup

115 G (4 OZ/½ CUP) *caster (superfine) sugar*
JUICE OF 1 *blood orange*
125 ML (4½ FL OZ/½ CUP) *water*
1 *cinnamon stick*
3 *cardamom pods,* GENTLY CRUSHED
2 TEASPOONS *orange blossom water*

To make the panna cotta, soak the gelatine leaves in a bowl of cold water for about 5 minutes to soften. Squeeze out the excess water. Meanwhile, place the cream, sugar and orange zest in a saucepan over medium–high heat. Gently bring to just below boiling point, remove from the heat, add the gelatine and stir to dissolve. Strain into a jug, discarding the zest. Pour the mixture into eight 125 ml (4 fl oz/½ cup) dariole moulds, cool to room temperature, and cover with plastic wrap. Transfer to the refrigerator and chill for 4 hours, or until set.

To make the syrup, place all the ingredients in a small saucepan over low heat and stir until the sugar has dissolved. Increase the heat to medium and simmer for 10 minutes, or until reduced to 100 ml (3½ fl oz). Strain the syrup into a jug and set aside to cool.

When ready to serve, remove from the refrigerator and invert each panna cotta onto a serving plate, drizzle the syrup over the top and decorate with pistachio nuts and serve with orange slices.

NOTE: You may substitute the gelatine leaves with 1½ teaspoons powdered gelatine combined with 2 tablespoons cold water. Microwave on high for 40–50 seconds, remove and stir until the gelatine dissolves. Also note, if blood oranges are unavailable you can use regular varieties of orange.

Greetings

Panettone *and* dark chocolate *bombe*

SERVES *8–10*
PREPARATION TIME *30 minutes, plus overnight freezing time and chilling time*
COOKING TIME *20 minutes*

900 G (2 LB) *panettone*
icing (confectioners') sugar, FOR DUSTING
300 G (10½ OZ) *raspberries,* TO SERVE

Dark chocolate ice cream
300 ML (10½ FL OZ) *thick cream*
200 G (7 OZ) *caster (superfine) sugar*
6 *egg yolks*
150 G (5½ OZ) *dark chocolate (70 per cent cocoa solids),* MELTED
550 ML (19 FL OZ) *milk*

To make the dark chocolate ice cream, place the cream and half the caster sugar in a saucepan over low heat and stir until the sugar has dissolved. Increase the heat, bring almost to boiling point and remove from the heat. Beat the egg yolks and the remaining caster sugar in a large bowl using electric beaters until pale and creamy. Whisk in the warm cream mixture, then return to the cleaned saucepan. Cook over medium heat, stirring constantly with a wooden spoon, until the mixture thickens slightly and coats the back of the spoon. Remove from the heat, whisk in the chocolate, then whisk in the milk. Pour into a jug or bowl, cover with plastic wrap and refrigerate until chilled. Churn in an ice-cream machine according to the manufacturer's instructions.

Meanwhile, invert the panettone onto a clean work surface and cut a circle in the base, leaving a 2 cm (¾ inch) border around the edge. Remove the disc of panettone and set aside. Hollow out the centre, leaving a 3–4 cm (1¼–1½ inch) wide shell of panettone. Place the panettone shell and disc in the freezer for 30 minutes to chill.

Spoon the ice cream into the panettone cavity using a spatula. Replace the base disc and invert the panettone onto a baking tray lined with baking paper. Cover the bombe with plastic wrap and freeze overnight, or until the ice cream is firm.

Transfer the panettone to a serving plate, pile the raspberries on top and dust with the icing sugar to serve. Cut the bombe into wedges.

Cakes *and* puddings

Serve up a slice of Christmas cheer with these seasonal staples.

Steamed Christmas pudding *with* caramel cream

SERVES *12–14*
PREPARATION TIME *30 minutes, plus 12 hours soaking time*
COOKING TIME *4 hours and 30 minutes*

250 G (9 OZ) *dried figs,* QUARTERED
200 G (7 OZ) *raisins*
150 G (5½ OZ) *sultanas (golden raisins)*
150 G (5½ OZ/1 CUP) *currants*
100 G (3½ OZ) *glacé (candied) cherries*
125 G (4½ OZ) *glacé (candied) ginger,* ROUGHLY CHOPPED
185 ML (6 FL OZ/¾ CUP) *brandy*
250 G (9 OZ/1 CUP) *butter,* SOFTENED
285 G (10 OZ/1¼ CUPS) *soft brown sugar*
2 TEASPOONS FINELY GRATED *orange zest*
3 *eggs*
50 G (1¾ OZ/⅓ CUP) *blanched almonds,* ROUGHLY CHOPPED
50 G (1¾ OZ/½ CUP) *pecans,* TOASTED AND ROUGHLY CHOPPED
180 G (6¼ OZ/2¼ CUPS) *fresh white breadcrumbs*
60 G (2¼ OZ/½ CUP) *plain (all-purpose) flour*
30 G (1 OZ/¼ CUP) *self-raising flour*
1 TEASPOON *mixed (pumpkin pie) spice*
1 TEASPOON *ground cinnamon*
rich custard sauce, TO SERVE (PAGE 198)

Caramel Cream

115 G (4 OZ/½ CUP) *caster (superfine) sugar*
250 ML (9 FL OZ/1 CUP) *cream*

Combine the figs, raisins, sultanas, currants, cherries and ginger in a large bowl, add the brandy and mix well. Cover the mixture and set aside to soak overnight.

Brush a 2.5 litre (87 fl oz/10 cup) pudding basin (mould) with melted butter and line the base with baking paper.

Beat the butter, sugar and orange zest in a large bowl with electric beaters until just combined. Add the eggs, one at a time, beating well after each addition. Stir in the nuts and combined breadcrumbs, flours, spices and the marinated fruit and mix thoroughly. Spoon the mixture into the prepared basin and smooth the surface with the back of a spoon. Tap gently on the work surface to release any air bubbles. Place a large sheet of foil on a work surface and cover with a sheet of baking paper. Grease the paper, make a pleat across the centre of both sheets, then wrap over the basin. Tie securely with kitchen string.

Place a small saucer on the base of a large saucepan and lower the pudding onto the saucer. Fill the saucepan with enough boiling water to come three-quarters up the side of the basin. Cover and simmer for 4½ hours, topping up with boiling water as necessary. Remove from the saucepan and stand for 5 minutes before turning out onto a serving plate.

Meanwhile, make the caramel cream. Place the sugar and 2 tablespoons water in a small heavy-based saucepan and cook, swirling occasionally, over medium–low heat for 4–5 minutes, or until a rich caramel colour. Remove from the heat, cool slightly, then add 80 ml (2½ fl oz/⅓ cup) of the cream. Return to the heat and stir over low heat until the caramel has dissolved and the sauce is smooth. Remove from the stovetop and allow to cool completely. Combine remaining cream with the caramel in a bowl and beat with electric beaters until soft peaks form.

Cut the into slices and serve with caramel cream and rich custard sauce.

Sticky ginger cake *with* white *frosting*

SERVES *8–10*
PREPARATION TIME *30 minutes*
COOKING TIME *1 hour, plus cooling time*

225 G (8 OZ) *self-raising flour*
1 TEASPOON *bicarbonate of soda (baking soda)*
1 TABLESPOON *ground ginger*
1 TEASPOON *ground cinnamon*
1 TEASPOON *mixed (pumpkin pie) spice*
115 G (4 OZ) *butter,* CHILLED AND CUT INTO CUBES
115 G (4 OZ/⅓ CUP) *dark muscovado sugar*
115 G (4 OZ/⅓ CUP) *black treacle (molasses)*
115 G (4 OZ/⅓ CUP) *golden syrup (light treacle)*
250 ML (9 FL OZ/1 CUP) *milk*
85 G (3 OZ) *preserved ginger,* DRAINED AND GRATED
1 *egg,* LIGHTLY BEATEN

White frosting

2 *egg whites*
½ TEASPOON *lemon juice*
1½ TEASPOONS *glycerine*
1 TEASPOON *orange liqueur* SUCH AS *Cointreau*
500 G (1 LB 2 OZ/4 CUPS) *icing (confectioners') sugar,* SIFTED

Preheat the oven to 180°C (350°F/Gas 4). Grease and line an 18 cm (7 inch) round cake tin.

Combine the flour, bicarbonate of soda and spices in a large mixing bowl, then rub in the butter until the mixture resembles fine breadcrumbs.

Place the sugar, treacle, golden syrup and milk in a saucepan and stir over low heat until the sugar has dissolved. Increase the heat and bring to just below boiling point.

Add the preserved ginger to the flour mixture and pour in the sugar mixture, stirring constantly with a wooden spoon until well combined. Add the egg and mix well. Pour into the prepared tin and bake for 55–60 minutes, or until a skewer inserted in the centre of the cake comes out clean. Allow to cool completely in the tin before turning out.

To make the white frosting, place the egg whites, lemon juice, glycerine and Cointreau in a large bowl, add one-third of the icing sugar and beat with electric beaters until well combined. Add the rest of the icing sugar and beat until white soft peaks form.

Evenly cover the cake with the white cream frosting using a small palette knife, and serve.

Stollen

SERVES *10–12*
PREPARATION TIME *30 minutes, plus 12 hours soaking time and 2 hours and 30 minutes rising time*
COOKING TIME *40 minutes, plus cooling time*

180 G (6¼ OZ) *raisins*
2½ TABLESPOONS *dark rum*
160 ML (5¼ FL OZ) *milk*, WARMED
2 TEASPOONS *dried yeast*
55 G (2 OZ/¼ CUP) *caster (superfine) sugar*
50 G (1¾ OZ/⅓ CUP) CHOPPED *blanched almonds*
625 G (1 LB 6 OZ/5 CUPS) *plain (all-purpose) flour*
¼ TEASPOON *ground cardamom*
¼ TEASPOON FRESHLY GRATED *nutmeg*
¼ TEASPOON *ground cinnamon*
250 G (9 OZ/1 CUP) *unsalted butter*, CUT INTO CUBES AND SOFTENED
1 *egg*
50 G (1¾ OZ) FINELY CHOPPED *glacé (candied) orange*
1 TEASPOON FINELY GRATED *lemon zest*
50 G (1¾ OZ) *unsalted butter*, MELTED
60 G (2¼ OZ/½ CUP) *icing (confectioners') sugar*, SIFTED

Place the raisins in a bowl, add the rum and mix well. Cover and set aside to soak overnight, then drain.

The next day, combine the milk, yeast and 1 tablespoon of the caster sugar in a small bowl. Set aside in a warm place for 10 minutes, or until frothy. Soak the almonds in boiling water for 10 minutes, drain.

Sift the flour, spices and the remaining caster sugar into a large bowl and make a well in the centre. Pour in the yeast mixture, add the butter and egg and mix with your hands until the dough just comes together. Turn out onto a lightly floured work surface and knead for 10–12 minutes, or until the dough is spongy and elastic. Sprinkle on the raisins, glacé orange, lemon zest and almonds and knead until soft and smooth. Transfer the dough to a large greased bowl and cover with plastic wrap. Place the bowl in a warm spot for 1½–2 hours, or until doubled in size.

Turn the dough out onto a lightly floured work surface, and knead and punch the dough, knocking all the air out of it. Shape into a 15 x 30 cm (6 x 12 inch) log, then wrap in foil (this helps the stollen keep its shape and prevents it from becoming flattened). Transfer the log to a baking tray, cover with a clean tea towel (dish towel) and set aside in a warm place for 30 minutes, or until light and puffy once more.

Preheat the oven to 180°C (350°F/Gas 4). Remove the foil and bake the stollen for 35–40 minutes, or until golden and well risen. Brush the top with the melted butter and dust with the icing sugar. Transfer to a wire rack to cool completely. Cut into 1 cm (½ inch) thick slices to serve.

NOTE: Stollen will keep, covered in foil and plastic wrap, in the refrigerator for up to 2 weeks.

Pumpkin *and* pecan roulade *with* ginger *cream*

SERVES *6*
PREPARATION TIME *20 minutes, plus 1 hour chilling time*
COOKING TIME *30 minutes, plus 30 minutes cooling time*

3 *eggs*
115 G (4 OZ/½ CUP) *soft brown sugar*
1 TEASPOON *natural vanilla extract*
90 G (3¼ OZ/⅓ CUP) *butter,* MELTED
125 G (4½ OZ/½ CUP) COOKED *mashed pumpkin (winter squash),* CHILLED
30 G (1 OZ/¼ CUP) *self-raising flour,* SIFTED
60 G (2¼ OZ/½ CUP) *plain (all-purpose) flour,* SIFTED
60 G (2¼ OZ/½ CUP) FINELY CHOPPED TOASTED *pecans*
icing (confectioners') sugar, FOR DUSTING

Ginger cream

150 ML (5 FL OZ) *cream (whipping)*
1 TABLESPOON *soft brown sugar*
LARGE PINCH OF *ground cinnamon*
2 TABLESPOONS FINELY CHOPPED *glacé (candied) ginger*

Ginger syrup

55 G (2 OZ/¼ CUP) *caster (superfine) sugar*
60 ML (2 FL OZ/¼ CUP) *green ginger wine*
1 TABLESPOON FINELY CHOPPED *glacé (candied) ginger*

To make the ginger cream, beat the cream, sugar and cinnamon in a bowl until firm peaks form, then fold in the ginger. Refrigerate until required.

To make the ginger syrup, combine the sugar, wine and ginger in a small saucepan and stir over low heat until the sugar has dissolved. Bring to the boil and simmer until syrupy. Remove from the heat and cool.

Preheat the oven to 180°C (350°F/Gas 4). Grease the base and sides of a 25 x 30 cm (10 x 12 inch) Swiss roll tin (jelly roll tin) and line the base and two opposite sides with baking paper. Cream the eggs, brown sugar and vanilla in a bowl using electric beaters until pale and fluffy. Fold in the butter, pumpkin and flours. Carefully spread the mixture into the prepared tin and bake for 12–15 minutes, or until a skewer inserted in the centre of the cake comes out clean.

Meanwhile, place a clean tea towel (dish towel) on a work surface, cover with a sheet of baking paper and sprinkle the pecans over the paper to form a rectangle the same size as the cake. Invert the cake onto the pecans and remove the lining paper. Using the remaining paper as a guide, roll up the cake lengthways and place, seam side down, on a wire rack to cool for 15 minutes. Carefully unroll and cool completely. Don't try to flatten the roll, leave it in a curved shape if necessary. When cold, spread the ginger cream over the cake and carefully roll up to enclose. Any cracks in the roulade can be gently eased together at this stage. Wrap firmly in plastic wrap and refrigerate for at least 1 hour.

To serve, cut the roulade into thick slices, drizzle with a little of the ginger syrup and dust lightly with the icing sugar.

Chocolate chestnut *puddings*

SERVES *12*
PREPARATION TIME *20 minutes*
COOKING TIME *1 hour and 15 minutes*

125 G (4½ OZ) FRESH *chestnuts*
250 G (9 OZ/1 CUP) *butter,* SOFTENED
345 G (12 OZ/1½ CUPS) *caster (superfine) sugar*
1 TEASPOON *natural vanilla extract*
2 *eggs*
2 *egg yolks*
185 G (6½ OZ/1½ CUPS) *plain (all-purpose) flour*
50 G (1¾ OZ) *unsweetened cocoa powder*
2 TEASPOONS *baking powder*
160 ML (5¼ FL OZ) *milk*
50 G (1¾ OZ) *dark chocolate,* CHOPPED

Chocolate sauce
125 ML (4 FL OZ/½ CUP) *cream*
125 G (4½ OZ) *dark chocolate,* FINELY CHOPPED

Preheat the oven to 180°C (350°F/Gas 4). Grease twelve 170 ml (5½ fl oz/⅔ cup) metal pudding basins (moulds), and line the bases with baking paper.

Score the chestnuts, place in a roasting tin and toast for 20–25 minutes, or until the shells start to separate. Remove from the oven and wrap in a clean tea towel (dish towel) for 5 minutes, then peel, removing the outer and inner skin. Set aside to cool, then finely chop.

Beat the butter, sugar and vanilla in a large bowl with electric beaters until pale and creamy. Add the eggs and egg yolks and beat well. Sift together the flour, cocoa and baking powder, then fold into the mixture with the milk until well combined and smooth. Fold in the chestnuts and chocolate and spoon into the prepared pudding basins. Place in a baking tin and pour in enough boiling water to come halfway up the side of the basins. Bake for 40–50 minutes, or until cooked through when tested with a skewer.

Meanwhile, to make the chocolate sauce, place the cream in a small saucepan and bring to the boil, add the chocolate and stir occasionally until melted.

To remove the puddings from the basins, carefully loosen around the edge with a small knife, gently tap the base and unmould onto serving plates. Serve with the chocolate sauce.

Apple *and* butterscotch *puddings*

MAKES *6*
PREPARATION TIME *20 minutes*
COOKING TIME *50 minutes, plus cooling time*

230 G (8¼ OZ/1 CUP) *caster (superfine) sugar*
500 ML (17 FL OZ/2 CUPS) *apple juice*
1 TABLESPOON *lemon juice*
2 STRIPS *lemon zest*
6 *small royal gala apples,* PEELED AND CORED

Pudding mixture

150 G (5½ OZ) *butter,* SOFTENED
80 G (2¾ OZ/⅓ CUP) *soft brown sugar*
2 TABLESPOONS *golden syrup (light treacle)*
2 *eggs*
2 TABLESPOONS *milk*
80 G (2¾ OZ) *plain (all-purpose) flour*
40 G (1½ OZ/⅓ CUP) *self-raising flour*
½ TEASPOON FRESHLY GRATED *nutmeg*

Butterscotch sauce

80 G (2¾ OZ/⅓ CUP) *soft brown sugar*
25 G (1 OZ) *butter*
125 ML (4 FL OZ/½ CUP) *cream*
1 TABLESPOON *brandy*

To poach the apples, combine the sugar, apple juice, lemon juice and zest and 500 ml (17 fl oz/2 cups) water in a large saucepan and stir over low heat until the sugar has dissolved. Bring to the boil, reduce the heat to low, add the apples in a single layer and cook, covered, for 10–15 minutes, or until just tender. Remove from the heat and allow the apples to cool in the syrup.

Preheat the oven to 180°C (350°F/Gas 4). Grease six 300 ml (10½ fl oz) ovenproof ramekins and line the bases with baking paper.

To make the pudding mixture, beat the butter, sugar and golden syrup in a large bowl using electric beaters until pale and fluffy. Add the eggs, one at a time, beating well after each addition. Fold in the milk, sifted flours and nutmeg in two batches. Divide half the mixture evenly among the prepared ramekins.

Drain the apples and pat dry with paper towels. Gently press an apple into each pudding and top with the remaining pudding mixture. Place the ramekins on a baking tray and bake for 35 minutes, or until the puddings are well browned and cooked when tested with a skewer. Allow the puddings to stand in the ramekins for 5 minutes before carefully removing. Place on serving plates and drizzle with the butterscotch sauce.

Meanwhile, make the butterscotch sauce. Sprinkle the sugar into a small heavy-based saucepan and cook, stirring occasionally, over medium heat until a deep caramel colour. Remove from the heat; add the butter and cream, taking care as the caramel will splatter. Place over low heat and cook, stirring frequently, for 10 minutes, or until the sauce is smooth and slightly thickened. Remove from the heat and stir in the brandy.

Bûche *de* Nöel

SERVES *8–10*
PREPARATION TIME *1 hour and 20 minutes*
COOKING TIME *1 hour and 40 minutes, plus cooling time*

Meringue mushrooms

3 *egg whites*
170 G (6 OZ/¾ CUP) *caster (superfine) sugar*
80 G (2¾ OZ) *dark chocolate,* MELTED

Cake

5 *eggs,* SEPARATED
115 G (4 OZ/½ CUP) *caster (superfine) sugar*
1 TEASPOON *natural almond extract*
125 G (4½ OZ/1 CUP) *plain (all-purpose) flour*

Praline

80 G (2¾ OZ/⅓ CUP) *caster (superfine) sugar*
50 G (1 ¾ OZ/⅓ CUP) BLANCHED *almonds*

Butter cream

55 G (2 OZ/¼ CUP) *caster (superfine) sugar*
2 *egg yolks*
280 G (10 OZ) *unsalted butter,* SOFTENED
100 G (3½ OZ) *dark chocolate,* MELTED, AT ROOM TEMPERATURE
2 TABLESPOONS *unsweetened cocoa powder,* SIFTED, PLUS EXTRA FOR DUSTING

Preheat the oven to 120°C (235°F/Gas ½). Line two baking trays with baking paper.

To make the meringue mushrooms, whisk the egg whites in a large bowl using electric beaters until stiff peaks form. Gradually add the sugar, a tablespoonful at a time, and whisk until the sugar has dissolved and the mixture is stiff and glossy. Transfer two-thirds of the mixture to a piping (icing) bag fitted with a 1 cm (½ inch) plain nozzle or a zip-lock bag with a small corner snipped off. Pipe twenty-five 3 cm (1¼ inch) rounds onto a prepared baking tray. To make the mushroom stems, place the remaining meringue in a small piping bag fitted with a 5 mm (¼ inch) plain nozzle or a zip-lock bag with a tiny corner snipped off. Pipe twenty-five 1 cm (½ inch) dollops onto the remaining baking tray. Bake for 1 hour, turn off the heat and leave the meringue to cool in the oven with the door slightly ajar (use a wooden spoon to prop the oven door open). Spread the underside of each mushroom cap with the melted chocolate and stick the 'peak' end of the meringue stems into the chocolate. Set aside to harden and set.

Preheat the oven to 190°C (375°F/Gas 5). Line a 25 x 30 cm (10 x 12 inch) Swiss roll tin (jelly roll tin) with baking paper, extending the paper over the long sides for easy removal later.

To make the cake, have all the ingredients at room temperature. Whisk the egg whites in a large bowl with electric beaters until firm peaks form. Beat the egg yolks, sugar and almond extract in a large bowl with electric beaters until pale and thick and tripled in volume. Sift in the flour and fold in with a metal spoon until just incorporated. Fold in the egg whites, taking care not to overmix. Spread the cake mixture into the prepared tin. Bake for 15 minutes, or until the surface springs back when touched. Invert the cake onto a clean tea towel, remove the lining paper and roll up lengthways, using the tea towel as a guide. Place the cake on a wire rack to cool completely.

To make the praline, combine the sugar and almonds in a small heavy-based saucepan and cook over low heat, stirring occasionally, until the sugar has dissolved. Increase the heat to medium and cook, without stirring, until golden. Pour onto a baking tray and spread out evenly using a wet spoon. Set aside to cool completely. Finely crush the praline using a rolling pin.

Meanwhile, to make the butter cream. Combine 60 ml (2 fl oz/¼ cup) water and the sugar in a small heavy-based saucepan over low heat and cook, stirring occasionally, until the sugar has dissolved. Increase the heat to medium–high, bring to the boil and cook, without stirring, until the temperature reaches 110°C (225°F) on a sugar (candy) thermometer. Place the egg yolks in a bowl and whisk, using electric beaters, while slowly pouring in the hot syrup in a thin steady stream. Continue beating for 3–5 minutes, or until the mixture has cooled. Add the butter and beat until smooth. Divide the butter cream in half and place in separate bowls. Stir the praline into one portion, then stir the melted chocolate and cocoa powder into the other.

Unroll the cake, spread on the praline butter cream, reserving 60 g (2¼ oz/¼ cup), and, using the tea towel, roll up lengthways into a log. Cut the ends of the log on the diagonal and reserve the trimmings for the branches. Dust a large serving plate with the extra cocoa. Transfer the log to the prepared plate. Place the trimmings on an angle on the log to form the branches. Spread the chocolate butter cream over the outside of the cake, leaving the cut ends uncovered. Smear the reserved praline butter cream over the uncovered ends of the log and branches. Run a fork along the length of the log to represent the bark and mark rings on the praline butter cream ends to represent the exposed cuts. Dust the plate with a little more cocoa to serve (see photograph, page 2).

NOTE: The finished cake can be made a day in advance and kept refrigerated. Then serve at room temperature.

Rich fig, prune *and* pecan *cake*

SERVES *12–16*
PREPARATION TIME *1 hour and 30 minutes, plus 12 hours soaking time and 1 week feeding the cake*
COOKING TIME *3 hours, plus cooling time*

400 G (14 OZ) *glacé (candied) fruit pineapple, peach, apricots, cherries,* CHOPPED
375 G (13 OZ) *pitted prunes,* CHOPPED
150 G (5½ OZ) *dried figs,* CHOPPED
250 G (9 OZ/2 CUPS) *raisins,* CHOPPED
125 ML (4 FL OZ/½ CUP) *brandy*
250 G (9 OZ/1 CUP) *unsalted butter,*
280 G (10 OZ/1½ CUPS) *dark brown sugar*
175 G (6 OZ/½ CUP) *golden syrup (light treacle)*
1 TABLESPOON *natural vanilla extract*
4 LARGE *eggs*
120 G (4¼ OZ/1 CUP) *pecans,* CHOPPED
2 TABLESPOONS *orange marmalade*
1 TABLESPOON FINELY GRATED *orange zest*
125 ML (4 FL OZ/½ CUP) FRESHLY SQUEEZED *orange juice*
345 G (12 OZ) *plain (all-purpose) flour*
1 TABLESPOON *baking powder,* SIFTED
1½ TABLESPOONS *ground cinnamon*
2 TEASPOONS FRESHLY GRATED *nutmeg*
2 TEASPOONS *ground ginger*
125 ML (4 FL OZ/½ CUP) *brandy,* EXTRA
70 CM (27½ INCH) SQUARE PIECE *muslin* (CHEESECLOTH)
icing (confectioners') sugar, SIFTED, FOR DUSTING

Place the glacé and dried fruit in a large bowl, add the brandy, cover and set aside to soak overnight.

Preheat the oven to 160°C (315°F/Gas 2–3). Lightly grease the base and sides of a 25 cm (10 inch) round cake tin and line with a double layer of baking paper.

Cream the butter and sugar in a large bowl with electric beaters until pale and fluffy. Add the golden syrup and vanilla and beat for 1 minute. Add the eggs, one at a time, beating well after each addition. Add the butter mixture to the fruit mixture, then stir in the pecans, marmalade and orange zest and juice. Fold in the sifted flour, baking powder, cinnamon, nutmeg and ginger until just combined.

Spoon the mixture into the prepared tin and smooth the surface with the back of a spoon. Tap the tin on the bench to release any air bubbles and level the surface with wet hands. Wrap the outside of the tin in two layers of brown paper and tie securely with kitchen string. Sit the cake on several layers of newspaper on the middle shelf in the oven. Bake for 2½–3 hours, covering the top of the cake with baking paper if browning too quickly. Test with a skewer to ensure that the cake is cooked through. Allow the cake to cool for 15 minutes. Pour 2 tablespoons of the extra brandy over the cake, cover the top of the cake with baking paper after 45 minutes and wrap in a clean tea towel (dish towel) until cold.

Soak the muslin in half the remaining brandy. Remove the cake from the tin and peel off the lining paper. Wrap the cake securely in the muslin and place in an airtight container. Pour a little of the remaining brandy over the cake every second day for seven days. When ready to serve, place a patterned doiley on top of the cake and dust with icing sugar. Carefully remove the doiley and serve.

Little fruit cake Christmas *tree*

MAKES *24 cakes*
PREPARATION TIME *40 minutes*
COOKING TIME *35 minutes, plus cooling time*

500 G (1 LB 2 OZ/4 CUPS) *raisins*
200 G (7 OZ) *glacé (candied) orange*, CHOPPED
300 G (10½ OZ) *sultanas (golden raisins)*
150 G (5½ OZ) *glacé (candied) cherries*, QUARTERED
150 G (5½ OZ) *butter*
165 G (5¾ OZ/¾ CUP) *soft brown sugar*
1 TABLESPOON FINELY GRATED *orange zest*
250 ML (9 FL OZ/1 CUP) FRESHLY SQUEEZED *orange juice*
125 ML (4 FL OZ/½ CUP) *Grand Marnier*
2 *eggs*, LIGHTLY BEATEN
2 TABLESPOONS *orange marmalade*
90 G (3¼ OZ/¾ CUP) *plain (all-purpose) flour*
90 G (3¼ OZ/¾ CUP) *self-raising flour*
55 G (2 OZ/½ CUP) *ground almonds*
1 TEASPOON FRESHLY GRATED *nutmeg*
2 TABLESPOONS *orange marmalade*, STRAINED
500 G (1 LB 2 OZ) *ready-rolled soft icing*
1 *egg white*
165 G (5¾ OZ/1⅓ CUPS) *icing (confectioners') sugar*
1 TEASPOON *lemon juice*
RED AND GREEN *food colouring*
Silver cachous AND *edible decorations*

Preheat the oven to 160°C (315°F/Gas 2–3). Line two 12-hole muffin tins with red, green and silver paper cases.

Combine the raisins, glacé orange, sultanas, glacé cherries, butter, brown sugar, orange zest and orange juice in a large saucepan and stir over low heat until the sugar has dissolved. Remove from the heat, stir in the Grand Marnier and allow to cool. When cold, stir in the egg and marmalade, then add the combined flours, ground almonds and nutmeg and mix well. Spoon the mixture into the prepared tins. Moisten your fingers with water and flatten the surface of each cake. Tap the tins firmly on the work surface to release any air bubbles. Bake for 30 minutes, or until a skewer inserted in the centre of a cake comes out clean. Remove from the oven, cover each tin with baking paper and wrap in a clean tea towel (dish towel). Allow the cakes to cool, then brush the tops lightly with the strained marmalade.

Roll out the icing until 3 mm (⅛ inch) thick and cut out twenty-four 6 cm (2½ inch) rounds. Place a round on top of each cake and smooth.

Whisk the egg white in a bowl until foamy. Gradually beat in the icing sugar and add just enough lemon juice to make a smooth icing that holds its shape. Divide the icing in half. Colour one batch green and the other red, then spoon each colour into a piping (icing) bag fitted with a 2 mm (1/16 inch) plain nozzle or into a zip-lock bag with a tiny corner snipped off. Pipe two green stripes (to represent the tree trunk) onto two cakes and pipe assorted green and red Christmas designs onto the remaining cakes.

To assemble the tree, using 17 of the cakes, place one cake at the top of a 40 x 50 cm (16 x 20 inch) covered cake board, then arrange the Christmas design cakes in rows in a triangular shape to represent a Christmas tree. Place the green striped cakes at the base to form the trunk.

Sour cherry, almond *and* white chocolate *pudding*

SERVES *10*
PREPARATION TIME *20 minutes*
COOKING TIME *2 hours and 5 minutes, plus cooling time*

340 G (11¾ OZ) *morello cherries*
60 ML (2 FL OZ/¼ CUP) *juice from cherries*
160 G (5¾ OZ/½ CUP) *cherry jam,* SIEVED
1 TABLESPOON *kirsch*
115 G (4 OZ/½ CUP) *caster (superfine) sugar*
100 G (3½ OZ) *butter,* SOFTENED
¼ TEASPOON *natural almond extract*
3 *eggs*
60 G (2¼ OZ/¼ CUP) *sour cream*
125 G (4½ OZ/1 CUP) *self-raising flour,* SIFTED
30 G (1 OZ/¼ CUP) *plain (all-purpose) flour,* SIFTED
70 G (2½ OZ/⅔ CUP) *ground almonds*
½ TEASPOON *baking powder,* SIFTED
80 G (2¾ OZ) *white chocolate,* FINELY CHOPPED
thick (double/heavy) cream, TO SERVE
25 G (1 OZ/¼ CUP) *toasted flaked almonds,* TO SERVE

Grease a 1.25 litre (44 fl oz/5 cup) metal pudding basin (mould) and cover the base with baking paper.

Combine the cherries, cherry juice, jam, kirsch and 2 tablespoons of the sugar in a small saucepan and stir over low heat until the sugar has dissolved. Strain, reserving the cherries and cherry syrup in separate bowls, and set aside to cool.

Cream the butter, the remaining sugar and the almond extract in a large bowl with electric beaters until pale and fluffy. Add the eggs, one at a time, beating well after each addition, then beat in the sour cream. Fold in the flours, ground almonds and baking powder. Fold in the chocolate, then add the reserved cherries.

Spoon the mixture into the prepared basin and smooth the top with the back of a spoon. Gently tap the basin on the work surface to release any air bubbles. Place a large sheet of foil on a work surface and cover with a sheet of baking paper. Grease the paper, make a pleat across the centre of both sheets, then wrap over the basin. Tie securely with kitchen string, leaving enough string to make a handle to lift the pudding out of the boiling water.

Place the pudding in a large saucepan and fill with enough boiling water to come three-quarters up the side of the basin. Cover and simmer, topping up with boiling water as necessary, for 2 hours, or until a skewer inserted in the centre of the pudding comes out clean. Allow the pudding to stand for 5 minutes before turning out onto a serving plate.

Serve slices of the pudding with the cream, almonds and the reserved cherry syrup.

Brown sugar and ginger rum *butter*

SERVES *8–10*
PREPARATION TIME *10 minutes, plus 2–3 hours chilling*

Beat 200 g (7 oz) diced and softened *butter*, 115 g (4 oz/ ½ cup) soft *brown sugar* and 1 teaspoon *mixed (pumpkin pie) spice* in a bowl using electric beaters until pale and fluffy. Gradually beat in 80 ml (2½ fl oz/⅓ cup) *dark rum* and fold in 55 g (2 oz/¼ cup) finely chopped *glacé (candied) ginger*. Transfer to a serving bowl, cover with plastic wrap and refrigerate until firm.

Orange brandy *butter*

SERVES *12*
PREPARATION TIME *15 minutes, plus 2 hours chilling*

Beat 250 g (9 oz/1 cup) softened *unsalted butter*, 2 teaspoons finely grated *orange zest*, 1 teaspoon *vanilla essence*, a pinch of *ground cinnamon*, a pinch of freshly *grated nutmeg*, 185 g (6½ oz/1½ cups) icing (confectioners') sugar and 2 tablespoons soft *brown sugar* in a large bowl using electric beaters until pale and fluffy. Add 2 tablespoons freshly squeezed *orange juice* and 80 ml (2½ fl oz/⅓ cup) *brandy* and beat for 2 minutes. Refrigerate in a sealed container until needed. Bring to room temperature before serving.

Bourbon and vanilla *sabayon*

MAKES *460 g (1 lb ½ oz/2 cups)*
PREPARATION TIME *5 minutes*
COOKING TIME *20 minutes*

Beat 6 *egg yolks*, 115 g (4 oz/½ cup) *caster (superfine) sugar* and 100 ml (3 ½ fl oz) *bourbon* in a large heatproof bowl using electric beaters until pale and creamy. Place over a saucepan of gently simmering water and continue to beat until the mixture thickens, triples in volume and forms a ribbon consistency. (Be careful not to let the water temperature increase to more than a gentle simmer as the eggs may scramble.) Remove from the heat, add 1 teaspoon *vanilla extract* and beat for 5 minutes. Bourbon and vanilla sabayon is best served immediately.

NOTE: The *bourbon* can be substituted with *dark rum*.

Rich custard *sauce*

SERVES *8–10*
PREPARATION TIME *5 minutes*
COOKING TIME *15 minutes*

Place 600 ml (21 fl oz) *cream*, 250 ml (9 fl oz/1 cup) *milk*, 60 ml (2 fl oz/¼ cup) *brandy* and 1 *vanilla bean*, split lengthways and seeds scraped, in a saucepan and gently bring to the boil over low–medium heat. Meanwhile, whisk 6 *egg yolks* and 145 g (5¼ oz/⅔ cup) *caster (superfine) sugar* in a large bowl using electric beaters until pale and very thick. Pour in the hot cream mixture and whisk to combine. Return to the cleaned saucepan and stir continuously over low–medium heat until the mixture thickens and coats the back of a wooden spoon. Remove from the heat, strain into a jug and serve immediately.

FROM TOP LEFT *Brown sugar and ginger rum* butter • *Orange brandy* butter
Bourbon and vanilla sabayon • *Rich custard* sauce

Drinks *and* nibbles

Get the festive season in full swing with our perfect party starters.

Mulled *wine*

SERVES *6* • PREPARATION TIME *5 minutes* • COOKING TIME *15 minutes*

1 *orange*
5 *cloves*
1.5 LITRES (52 FL OZ/6 CUPS) *red wine*
1 *cinnamon stick*
1 *nutmeg*
200 G (7 OZ) *caster (superfine) sugar*
200 ML (7 FL OZ) *brandy*

Stud the orange with the cloves and place all the ingredients in a large saucepan. Add 250 ml (9 fl oz/1 cup) water and simmer for 10–15 minutes, stirring until the sugar has dissolved. Do not allow the liquid to boil as the wine will evaporate.

Strain into a large jug and serve warm.

Vanilla *and* nutmeg *martini*

SERVES *6* • PREPARATION TIME *5 minutes, plus 1 hour chilling time*

240 ML (8 FL OZ) *gin*
1 *vanilla bean,* SPLIT LENGTHWAYS AND *seeds* SCRAPED
115 G (4 OZ/½ CUP) *caster (superfine) sugar*
1 TEASPOON FRESHLY GRATED *nutmeg*
2 TABLESPOONS *Cointreau*
2 TABLESPOONS *dry vermouth*
135 G (4¾ OZ/1 CUP) *ice cubes,* CRUSHED

Chill the gin and six martini glasses in the freezer for at least 1 hour.

Place the vanilla seeds, sugar and nutmeg on a plate and mix well.

Combine the gin, Cointreau, vermouth and ice in a jug or cocktail shaker and stir. Press rims of the chilled glasses onto the spiced sugar then strain 5 tablespoons of the gin mixture into each glass. Serve immediately.

Spiced *nuts*

SERVES *10–12*
PREPARATION TIME *5 minutes*
COOKING TIME *10 minutes*

125 G (4½ OZ) *whole almonds*
125 G (4½ OZ) *cashew nuts*
125 G (4½ OZ) *pecans*
125 G (4½ OZ) *hazelnuts,* TOASTED AND SKINNED
1 TABLESPOON *sea salt*
½ TEASPOON *cayenne pepper*
30 G (1 OZ) *unsalted butter*
2½ TEASPOONS *soft brown sugar*
2 TEASPOONS CHOPPED *rosemary*

Preheat the oven to 200°C (400°F/Gas 6).

Place the nuts on a baking tray and toast for 5–7 minutes, or until aromatic. Remove from the oven and sprinkle on the salt and cayenne pepper.

Melt the butter and sugar in a large saucepan and stir to combine. Add the nuts and rosemary and stir to coat. Set aside to cool slightly. Serve warm or at room temperature.

Parmesan *and* thyme *wafers*

MAKES *18*
PREPARATION TIME *5 minutes*
COOKING TIME *10 minutes*

125 G (4½ OZ/1¼ CUPS) FINELY GRATED *parmesan cheese*
3 TEASPOONS *thyme leaves*

Preheat the oven to 180°C (350°F/Gas 4). Line two baking trays with baking paper. Combine the parmesan and thyme in a bowl.

Place 2 tablespoons of the mixture on the prepared trays and shape into rough rectangles.

Bake for 8–10 minutes, or until light golden. Cool on the trays then break into smaller pieces.

Champagne *oysters*

SERVES *4*
PREPARATION TIME *10 minutes*
COOKING TIME *30 minutes*

1 *French shallot,* FINELY CHOPPED
150 ML (10½ FL OZ) *Champagne or sparkling white wine*
150 G (5½ OZ) *unsalted butter,* CUT INTO CUBES
2 TABLESPOONS *crème fraîche*
2 *egg yolks*
500 G (1 LB 2 OZ) *rock salt*
24 *oysters,* ON THE SHELL

Combine the shallot and 125 ml (4 fl oz/½ cup) of the Champagne or sparkling white wine in a small saucepan over medium heat and simmer until reduced to 1 tablespoon. Strain the liquid into a heatproof bowl, discarding the shallot. Place the bowl over a saucepan of gently simmering water and whisk in the butter, one piece at a time, until thick and creamy. Remove from the heat and stir in the crème fraîche.

Place the egg yolks and the remaining Champagne in a separate heatproof bowl over a saucepan of gently simmering water and whisk until the mixture forms ribbons when drizzled. (Be careful not to scramble the egg.) Remove from the heat and fold into the butter mixture. Season lightly with sea salt and freshly ground black pepper.

Preheat the grill (broiler) to medium–high. Spread the rock salt on a baking tray and arrange the oysters on the salt bed. Spoon a teaspoon of the Champagne mixture onto each oyster and cook 10 cm (4 inches) from the heat for 1–2 minutes, or until golden brown. Serve immediately.

Seafood tartlets *with* dill *mayonnaise*

MAKES *36*
PREPARATION TIME *30 minutes, plus 2 hours chilling time*
COOKING TIME *40 minutes*

- 155 G (5½ OZ/1¼ CUPS) *plain (all-purpose) flour*
- 100 G (3½ OZ) *unsalted butter,* CHILLED AND CUT INTO CUBES
- 2 TABLESPOONS *sour cream*
- 160 G (5¾ OZ/⅔ CUP) *mayonnaise*
- 2 TABLESPOONS *lemon juice*
- 1 TABLESPOON FINELY CHOPPED *dill,* PLUS EXTRA TO GARNISH
- 1 TABLESPOON FINELY SNIPPED *chives*
- 400 G (14 OZ) PEELED, *cooked prawns* OR COOKED *lobster tail,* SLICED

Place the flour and butter in the bowl of a food processor and process until the mixture resembles fine breadcrumbs. Add the sour cream and pulse to combine. Add 1½ tablespoons cold water and pulse until the pastry just comes together.

Turn the pastry out onto a lightly floured work surface. Press into a ball and flatten into a disc. Cover with plastic wrap and refrigerate for 2 hours, or until required.

Preheat oven to 180°C (350°F/Gas 4). Roll out the pastry between two sheets of baking paper until 2 mm (1/16 inch) thick. Then, use a 5 cm (2 inch) cutter to cut rounds from the pastry. Press 12 rounds into a 12-hole mini muffin tin, place another muffin tin on top to weigh it down and refrigerate the remaining rounds until required. Bake for 6 minutes, then remove the top muffin tin, return to the oven and bake for a further 6 minutes, or until the pastry is golden and crisp. Remove the tartlets from the tin and repeat with the remaining pastry rounds. Allow to cool.

Combine the mayonnaise, lemon juice and herbs in a small bowl. Spoon teaspoons of the mayonnaise mixture into the tartlet shells, top with a slice of prawn or lobster and sprinkle with the extra dill. Serve immediately.

Quail eggs *with* spiced *salt*

SERVES *8–12*
PREPARATION TIME *5 minutes*
COOKING TIME *20 minutes, plus cooling time*

24 *quail eggs*
½ TEASPOON *fennel seeds*
¼ TEASPOON *caraway seeds*
1 TABLESPOON *sea salt*
PINCH OF *sweet paprika*

Bring a small saucepan of salted water to the boil. Add the quail eggs and cook in batches of four for 3 minutes. Remove from the water with a slotted spoon and plunge into iced water. Peel the eggs immediately and set aside to cool.

Place the fennel and caraway seeds in a small saucepan over high heat and cook until fragrant and popping. Finely grind using a mortar and pestle, then mix with the sea salt and paprika. Peel eggs and serve with the seasoned salt on the side.

Rhubarb *and* cinnamon *martini*

SERVES *8* • PREPARATION TIME *10 minutes* • COOKING TIME *20 minutes, plus cooling time*

crushed ice
500 ML (17 FL OZ/2 CUPS) *vodka*, CHILLED
80 ML (2½ FL OZ/⅓ CUP) *orange liqueur*, SUCH AS *Grand Marnier*
2 TABLESPOONS *lemon juice*

Rhubarb purée
400 G (14 OZ) *rhubarb*, TRIMMED AND CHOPPED
115 G (4 OZ/½ CUP) *caster (superfine) sugar*
125 ML (4 FL OZ/½ CUP) *orange juice*
2 *cinnamon sticks*

To make the rhubarb purée, place the rhubarb, sugar, orange juice and cinnamon sticks in a saucepan over low heat and simmer for 20 minutes. Set aside to cool. Remove the cinnamon sticks and blend the rhubarb until smooth. You should have 330 ml (11¼ fl oz/1⅓ cups) of purée.

For the best result, make one cocktail at a time. Half fill a cocktail shaker with ice, top with 40 ml (1¼ fl oz) rhubarb purée, 60 ml (2 fl oz/¼ cup) vodka, 2 teaspoons orange liqueur and 1 teaspoon lemon juice. Shake and strain into a chilled martini glass to serve. Repeat to make eight martinis.

Pear *and* ginger Champagne *cocktail*

SERVES *6* • PREPARATION TIME *5 minutes, plus chilling time* • COOKING TIME *35 minutes*

230 G (8¼ OZ/1 CUP) *caster (superfine) sugar*
6 CM (2½ INCH) PIECE *fresh ginger*, PEELED AND CUT INTO DICE
185 ML (6 FL OZ/¾ CUP) *100 per cent pear juice*
750 ML (26 FL OZ/3 CUPS) *Champagne or sparkling white wine*

Place the sugar, ginger and 250 ml (9 fl oz/1 cup) water in a small saucepan and cook, stirring occasionally, over low heat until the sugar has dissolved. Increase the heat and simmer for 30 minutes, or until syrupy and reduced by half. Remove from the heat, strain and set aside to cool. Cover and refrigerate to chill.

When ready to serve, place the pear juice and 80 ml (2½ fl oz/⅓ cup) of the ginger syrup in a jug and stir to combine. Evenly distribute between six cocktail glasses. Top with the Champagne or sparkling wine and serve.

TIP: Any left-over syrup will keep, stored in an airtight container, in the refrigerator for up to 2 weeks.

Parmesan puffs *with* crabmeat *cream*

MAKES *40–45*
PREPARATION TIME *20 minutes*
COOKING TIME *40 minutes, plus cooling time*

Parmesan puffs

100 G (3½ OZ) *unsalted butter*
½ TEASPOON *salt*
130 G (4¾ OZ) *plain (all-purpose) flour,* SIFTED
3 *eggs*
25 G (1 OZ/¼ CUP) FINELY GRATED *parmesan cheese*
1 *egg* LIGHTLY BEATEN WITH 1 TABLESPOON *milk,* TO GLAZE

Crabmeat cream

200 G (7 OZ) *cream cheese,* AT ROOM TEMPERATURE
4 TABLESPOONS *sour cream*
2 *spring onions (scallions), white and green part,* THINLY SLICED
½ TEASPOON FINELY GRATED *lemon zest*
1 TEASPOON *lemon juice*
Tabasco sauce, TO TASTE
150 G (5½ OZ) COOKED *crabmeat,* FINELY SHREDDED

Preheat the oven to 200°C (400°F/Gas 6). Grease two baking trays.

To make the parmesan puffs, combine the butter, salt and 250 ml (9 fl oz/ 1 cup) water in a saucepan over medium–high heat and bring to the boil. Remove from the heat, add the flour all at once and stir with a wooden spoon to combine. Return to the heat and cook, stirring constantly, over medium heat until the mixture comes away from the side and base of the pan, forming a ball around the spoon. Remove from the heat. Stir in the eggs, one at a time, making sure each is well incorporated and the mixture comes away from the side of the pan after each addition. Stir in the parmesan. Drop teaspoons of the dough onto the prepared trays. Brush the tops with the egg glaze. Bake for 6–8 minutes, or until puffed. Reduce the temperature to 180°C (350°F/Gas 4) and bake for a further 20 minutes to dry out and brown. Turn the puffs out onto a wire rack and pierce each one with a knife point to release steam. Allow to cool completely.

To make the crabmeat cream, combine the cream cheese, sour cream, spring onion, lemon zest and lemon juice in a small bowl and add the Tabasco sauce. Fold in the crabmeat.

Cut the puffs in half horizontally, leaving a hinge, and fill the base with 1 teaspoon of the filling. Flip the top half over the filling, place on a platter and serve immediately.

NOTES: The puffs can be made ahead and stored, unfilled, in an airtight container, for up to 2 days. Reheat in a 180°C (350°F/Gas 4) oven for 5 minutes to crisp up.

Replace the crabmeat in the filling with 100 g (3½ oz) shredded smoked trout, if preferred, or half of each.

Duck liver *parfait* *with* spiced pear *chutney*

SERVES *10–12*
PREPARATION TIME *40 minutes, plus 4 hours marinating time and 12 hours chilling time*
COOKING TIME *1 hour, plus cooling time*

500 G (1 LB 2 OZ) *duck livers,* TRIMMED
125 ML (4 FL OZ/½ CUP) *Madeira*
2 TABLESPOONS *Cognac or brandy*
5 *thyme sprigs*
1 *garlic clove,* CRUSHED
1 *French shallot,* FINELY CHOPPED
200 G (7 OZ) *unsalted butter,* SOFTENED
3 *eggs*
80 ML (2½ FL OZ/⅓ CUP) *cream*
1 TEASPOON *Chinese five-spice*
1 TEASPOON *sea salt*
PINCH OF *white pepper*
TOASTED *brioche,* TO SERVE

Spiced pear chutney

1 TABLESPOON *olive oil*
1 *red onion,* FINELY CHOPPED
½ TEASPOON *Chinese five-spice*
2 *beurre bosc pears,* PEELED, CORED AND VERY FINELY DICED
115 G (4 OZ/½ CUP) *soft brown sugar*
60 ML (2 FL OZ/¼ CUP) *cider vinegar*
60 ML (2 FL OZ/¼ CUP) *white wine*

Combine the livers, Madeira, cognac or brandy, thyme, garlic and shallot in a bowl, cover and refrigerate for 4 hours. Drain, reserving the marinade. Set aside the livers.

Transfer the marinade to a small saucepan and simmer over medium heat for 8 minutes, or until reduced to 80 ml (2½ fl oz/⅓ cup). Strain the marinade to remove the solids.

Preheat the oven to 120°C (235°F/Gas ½). Grease a 1.25 litre (52 fl oz/ 6 cup) terrine tin and line with baking paper.

Pat the livers dry. Melt 50 g (1¾ oz) of the butter in a saucepan over medium–high heat. Add the livers and cook for 3 minutes on each side, or until browned but still rare inside. Remove and allow to cool.

Cut the remaining butter into small pieces. Place the livers in the bowl of a food processor and process until smooth. Add the eggs, cream, the reduced marinade and the chopped butter and process until combined. Pass the mixture through a sieve into a large bowl, add the Chinese five-spice and salt and pepper and transfer to the prepared tin, smoothing the surface with the back of a spoon.

Place the terrine in a large roasting tin and pour in enough boiling water to come halfway up the sides of the terrine tin. Cook for 45 minutes, or until a metal skewer inserted in the centre of the terrine is warm to the touch. Remove from the water bath and set aside to cool. Cover with plastic wrap and refrigerate overnight.

Meanwhile, make the spiced pear chutney. Heat the oil in a saucepan over medium heat, add the onion and cook, stirring often, for 5 minutes, or until soft. Add the remaining ingredients and simmer for 40 minutes, or until thick. Allow to cool.

Turn the parfait out onto a serving platter and serve with the chutney and toasted brioche.

Caramelised leek *and* stilton *pastries*

MAKES *30*
PREPARATION TIME *20 minutes, plus 1 hour chilling time*
COOKING TIME *30 minutes, plus cooling time*

15 G (1/2 OZ) *unsalted butter*
2 TABLESPOONS *olive oil*
1 *leek,* WHITE PART ONLY, FINELY CHOPPED
100 G (3 1/2 OZ) *stilton cheese,* CUT INTO 30 SMALL PIECES
30 G (1 OZ) *prosciutto,* FINELY DICED
1 *egg*
1 TABLESPOON *water*

Pastry
250 G (4 1/2 OZ/1 CUP) *plain (all-purpose) flour*
200 G (3 1/2 OZ) *unsalted butter,* CHILLED AND CUT INTO CUBES
120 G (2 1/4 OZ/1/4 CUP) *sour cream*

To make the pastry, combine all the ingredients in the bowl of a food processor and pulse until just combined. Remove the dough and form into a disc. Cover with plastic wrap and refrigerate for at least 1 hour.

Heat the butter and oil in a frying pan over medium heat. Add the leek and cook, stirring occasionally, for 20 minutes, or until soft and golden brown. Season with freshly ground black pepper and set aside to cool.

Preheat the oven to 200°C (400°F/Gas 6). Line two baking trays with baking paper.

Roll out half the pastry on a lightly floured work surface to form a 30 x 40cm (12 x 16 inch) rectangle. Use a 7 cm (2 3/4 inch) cutter to cut out rounds from the pastry. Bring the pastry scraps together, roll and cut out rounds again, as necessary. Repeat with the remaining pastry.

Place 1 teaspoon of the caramelised leek in the centre of each pastry round. Top with a piece of stilton and a little prosciutto.

Whisk the egg and water in a small bowl. Brush the pastry edges with the egg wash. Fold the pastry over the filling to form a semicircle, then seal the edges. Transfer to the prepared trays. Brush the pastry tops with a little egg wash and bake for 8–10 minutes, or until golden. Serve warm.

NOTE: The pastries can be prepared ahead and covered and refrigerated until required. Alternatively, the cooked pastries can be frozen. Thaw before reheating in a 120°C (235°F/Gas 1/2) oven for 10 minutes.

Pomegranate *and* rosewater *martini*

SERVES *6* • PREPARATION TIME *5 minutes*

1 *pomegranate*
280 ML (9¾ FL OZ) *vodka,* CHILLED
1 TABLESPOON *rosewater*
135 G (4¾ OZ/1 CUP) *ice cubes,* CRUSHED

Cut the pomegranate in half, remove the seeds and squeeze the juice into a small bowl.

Place eight pomegranate seeds and 1 teaspoon of the reserved pomegranate juice in each of six chilled martini glasses.

Combine the vodka, rosewater, and ice in a jug or cocktail shaker and stir. Strain over the pomegranate seeds and juice.

Hazelnut *and* lime Champagne *cocktail*

SERVES *4* • PREPARATION TIME *5 minutes*

2 TABLESPOONS *lime juice*
1 TABLESPOON *caster (superfine) sugar*
80 ML (2½ FL OZ/⅓ CUP) *hazelnut liqueur,* SUCH AS *Frangelico*
Champagne or sparkling white wine

Combine the lime juice and sugar in a small bowl and stir until all of the sugar dissolves.

Divide the lime mixture and Frangelico among four cocktail glasses. Top with the Champagne or sparkling wine and serve.

Cheese *twists*

MAKES *16*
PREPARATION TIME *10 minutes, plus 30 minutes chilling time*
COOKING TIME *25 minutes*

- 40 G (1½ OZ) *Boursin* OR *herbed cream cheese,* AT ROOM TEMPERATURE
- 2 SHEETS *frozen puff pastry,* THAWED
- 30 G (1 OZ/¼ CUP) FINELY GRATED *tasty cheese*
- 2 TABLESPOONS FINELY GRATED *parmesan cheese*
- 2 TABLESPOONS FINELY SNIPPED *chives*
- 1 TABLESPOON *milk*

Preheat the oven to 220°C (425°F/Gas 7). Line two baking trays with baking paper.

Spread the Boursin cheese over the pastry. Sprinkle one sheet of pastry with the combined grated cheeses and chives, then place the other sheet on top, pressing down firmly to join. Lightly brush the pastry with the milk and sprinkle with sea salt. Cut evenly into 16 thin strips. Twist the strips three or four times and place on the prepared trays. Refrigerate for 30 minutes. Bake for 20–25 minutes, or until golden brown. Cool on a wire rack.

Salmon pâté *with* toasts

SERVES *8–10*
PREPARATION TIME *10 minutes, plus 12 hours chilling time*
COOKING TIME *5 minutes, plus cooling time*

60 ML (2 FL OZ/¼ CUP) *white wine*
250 ML (9 FL OZ/1 CUP) *fish stock*
2 *garlic cloves,* PEELED
1 *bay leaf*
500 G (1 LB 2 OZ) *salmon fillet,* SKIN AND BONES REMOVED, CUT INTO LARGE CUBES
200 G (7 OZ) *unsalted butter,* SOFTENED
2 TABLESPOONS CHOPPED *dill*
100 G (3½ OZ) *smoked salmon*
1 TABLESPOON *lemon juice*
1 *baguette,* CUT INTO 1 CM (½ INCH) THICK SLICES, TOASTED
salmon roe, TO SERVE

Combine the wine, stock, garlic and bay leaf in a saucepan and bring to the boil. Reduce the heat to low, add the salmon and poach for 1–2 minutes, or until the salmon is just cooked. Remove the salmon with a slotted spoon, place on a plate and set aside to cool.

When cool enough to handle, transfer the salmon to the bowl of a food processor. Add the butter, dill and smoked salmon and process until just combined, leaving a little texture. Season with sea salt and freshly ground black pepper and add lemon juice to taste.

Spoon the mixture into a 500 ml (17 fl oz/2 cup) ceramic dish. Cover and refrigerate overnight. Bring to room temperature before serving.

To serve, spread the slices of the toasted baguette with the salmon pâté and top with a little of the salmon roe.

Creamed salt cod *with* potato crisps

SERVES *8*
PREPARATION TIME *30 minutes, plus 24 hours soaking time*
COOKING TIME *40 minutes*

500 G (1 LB 2 OZ) *dried salt cod*
100 G (3½ OZ) *all-purpose potato,* SUCH AS SPUNTA OR DESIREE
1 LITRE (35 FL OZ/4 CUPS) *milk*
1 *bay leaf*
1 TEASPOON *black peppercorns*
2 *garlic cloves,* CRUSHED
200 ML (3½ FL OZ) *extra virgin olive oil*
120 ML (2 FL OZ/¼ CUP) *thick cream*
1 TABLESPOON FINELY CHOPPED *flat-leaf (Italian) parsley*

Potato crisps
4 *russet (roasting) potatoes*
canola or vegetable oil, FOR DEEP FRYING
paprika, FOR DUSTING

Place the cod in a glass bowl and cover with water. Soak for 24 hours, changing the water three times.

Cook the potato in boiling water for 15 minutes, or until very tender. Drain, and when cool enough to handle, peel and mash the potato until very smooth.

Meanwhile, drain the cod and place in a saucepan. Add the milk, bay leaf and peppercorns and simmer for 10 minutes, or until the cod flesh falls apart easily. Drain, remove and discard the bones, bay leaf and peppercorns. Flake the cod flesh and mix into the potato with the garlic.

Warm the oil and cream in a small saucepan over low heat.

Beat the warmed cream mixture into the potato and cod mixture with a wooden spoon. Continue beating until all the liquid is incorporated, the fish is in small threads and the mixture is creamy. Season with freshly ground black pepper and stir in the parsley. Transfer to a serving bowl.

Preheat the oven to 100°C (200°F/Gas ½).

To make the potato crisps, slice the potatoes as thinly as possible. Place the potato in a large bowl of cold water to prevent discolouring. Pour the oil into a deep-fryer or a large heavy-based saucepan to a depth of 5 cm (2 inches). Heat until hot, about 180°C (350°F), or until a cube of bread dropped into the oil browns in 15 seconds. Drain the potato and pat dry with paper towel. Cook the potato, in small batches, for 1–2 minutes, or until golden. Use a slotted spoon or strainer to transfer the crisps to a large bowl lined with paper towel. Keep warm in the oven and repeat with the remaining potato. Transfer to warmed serving plates, sprinkle on sea salt and the paprika and serve with the cod for dipping or spooning on.

NOTE: The creamed salt cod can be made several hours ahead. Store, covered, in the refrigerator until required. Serve at room temperature.

Cranberry *and* apple *martini*

SERVES *6* • PREPARATION TIME *10 minutes*

60 ML (2 FL OZ/$^1/_4$ CUP) *dry vermouth*
crushed ice
185 ML (6 FL OZ/$^3/_4$ CUP) *gin*
1$^1/_2$ TABLESPOONS *apple schnapps*
270 ML (9$^1/_2$ FL OZ) *cloudy apple juice*
90 ML (3 FL OZ) *cranberry juice*
6 *apple slices,* SUCH AS ROYAL GALA, TO SERVE

For the best result, mix one cocktail at a time. Pour 2 teaspoons of vermouth into a chilled martini glass and swirl to coat the sides. Discard the remaining liquid.

Half fill a cocktail shaker with the crushed ice, add 2$^1/_2$ tablespoons of gin, 1 teaspoon of apple schnapps, 45 ml (1$^1/_2$ fl oz) of apple juice and 3 teaspoons of cranberry juice. Stir and strain into the glass, garnish with a slice of apple. Repeat to make six martinis.

Blood orange Champagne *cocktail*

SERVES *4* • PREPARATION TIME *5 minutes*

125 ML (4 FL OZ/$^1/_2$ CUP) *Campari*
125 ML (4 FL OZ/$^1/_2$ CUP) *blood orange juice*
Champagne or sparkling white wine

Divide the Campari and orange juice among four cocktail glasses. Top with Champagne or sparkling wine and serve.

Merry Christmas

Edible gifts

In the spirit of giving, create some delectable decorations and treats for friends and family.

Raspberry *and* white chocolate *truffles*

MAKES *24*
PREPARATION TIME *1 hour, plus 5 hours setting time*
COOKING TIME *10 minutes*

500 G (1 LB 2 OZ) *white chocolate,* ROUGHLY CHOPPED
125 ML (4 FL OZ/½ CUP) *thick cream*
1 TABLESPOON FINELY GRATED *lemon zest*
24 *raspberries*
icing (confectioners') sugar, SIFTED, FOR DUSTING

Place half the chocolate in a heatproof bowl. Combine the cream and lemon zest in a small saucepan over medium heat and bring almost to the boil. Remove from the heat and swirl the pan to mix well. Pour the cream mixture over the chocolate and stir until the chocolate has melted. Place the bowl over a saucepan of simmering water if the chocolate does not melt completely. Allow to cool to room temperature, then place in the refrigerator for 3 hours, or until set but still pliable.

Line a tray with baking paper. Working quickly, flatten a tablespoon of the chocolate mixture in the palm of your hands. Place a raspberry in the centre, wrap the chocolate around it and roll it into a ball. Transfer to the prepared tray. Repeat, using all of the mixture. Return to the refrigerator for 1 hour.

Meanwhile, place the remaining chocolate in a heatproof bowl. Half fill a saucepan with water, bring to the boil and remove from the heat. Sit the bowl over the saucepan, making sure the base of the bowl doesn't touch the water. Stand, stirring occasionally, until the chocolate has melted. Remove the bowl from the saucepan.

Dip the balls, one by one, in the melted chocolate and roll until they are completely covered. Use two small spoons to remove each ball from the chocolate and return to the tray. Repeat until all the balls are coated in chocolate. Transfer to the refrigerator for 1 hour to set. Dust with the icing sugar and serve.

Rum and raisin *balls*

MAKES *45*
PREPARATION TIME *30 minutes, plus 1 hour soaking time and 1 hour and 30 minutes setting time*

60 G (2¼ OZ/½ CUP) *raisins*
80 ML (2½ FL OZ/⅓ CUP) *dark rum*
500 G (1 LB 2 OZ) PURCHASED *madeira (pound) cake*
250 G (9 OZ) GOOD-QUALITY *marzipan*
375 G (13 OZ/2½ CUPS) *dark chocolate melts,* MELTED
30 G (1 OZ/¼ CUP) SLIVERED *almonds,* LIGHTLY TOASTED

Line two trays with baking paper.

Combine the raisins and rum in a small bowl and set aside for 1 hour. Strain the rum into a small bowl and set aside. Place the raisins in a separate small bowl.

Trim and discard any dark edges from the cake. Place the cake, marzipan and reserved rum in the bowl of a food processor and process until just combined. Transfer to a bowl and stir in the raisins.

Roll heaped teaspoons of the mixture into balls, place on the prepared trays and refrigerate for 1 hour, or until firm. Roll the balls in the chocolate using your fingertips and return to the trays for 30 minutes, or until the chocolate is almost set. Top with slivered almonds and allow to set.

Pistachio macaroons *with* lemon *cream*

MAKES *20*
PREPARATION TIME *25 minutes, plus standing time and setting time*
COOKING TIME *15 minutes*

125 G ($4\frac{1}{2}$ OZ/1 CUP) *icing (confectioners') sugar*
80 G ($2\frac{3}{4}$ OZ/$\frac{1}{2}$ CUP) *pistachio nuts*
3 *egg whites*
PINCH OF *salt*
2 TABLESPOONS *caster (superfine) sugar*
PINCH OF *cream of tartar*
icing (confectioners') sugar, SIFTED, FOR DUSTING

Lemon cream

150 G ($5\frac{1}{2}$ OZ) *white chocolate,* ROUGHLY CHOPPED
100 ML ($3\frac{1}{2}$ FL OZ) *cream*
1 TEASPOON FINELY GRATED *lemon zest*

Line two baking trays with baking paper.

Place the icing sugar and pistachio nuts in the bowl of a food processor and process until the mixture resembles fine breadcrumbs.

Beat the egg whites and salt in a large bowl using electric beaters until soft peaks form. Gradually add the caster sugar and beat until the mixture is thick and glossy and the sugar has dissolved. Fold in the cream of tartar, then gently fold in the pistachio mixture. Spoon teaspoons of the mixture onto the prepared trays and allow to stand at room temperature for 30 minutes.

Preheat the oven to 120°C (235°F/Gas 1–2). Bake the macaroons for 10–12 minutes. Allow to cool on the trays.

Meanwhile, to make the lemon cream, combine the chocolate and cream in a small saucepan and place over low heat, stirring with a metal spoon, until the chocolate has melted. Transfer to a bowl, stir in the lemon zest, then refrigerate until set.

Spread the lemon cream on the base of half the macaroons. Sandwich together, dust with icing sugar and serve.

Merry

FINAL
SPECIAL

Vanilla *and* spice *marshmallows*

MAKES *25*
PREPARATION TIME *40 minutes, plus overnight setting time*
COOKING TIME *20 minutes*

2 TEASPOONS *natural vanilla extract*
15 G (1/2 OZ) *powdered gelatine*
1/2 TEASPOON *ground cinnamon*
1/4 TEASPOON FRESHLY GRATED *nutmeg*
330 G (11 1/2 OZ/1 1/2 CUPS) *sugar*
100 G (3 1/2 OZ) *corn syrup*
85 G (3 OZ/2/3 CUP) *icing (confectioners') sugar*
60 G (2 1/4 OZ/1/2 CUP) *cornflour (cornstarch)*

Line the base and sides of a 20 cm (8 inch) square cake tin with baking paper and lightly spray with oil.

Combine the vanilla and 80 ml (2 1/2 fl oz/1/3 cup) water in a large bowl, sprinkle the gelatine and spices over the top and set aside for 10 minutes.

Combine the sugar, corn syrup and 80 ml (2 1/2 fl oz/1/3 cup) water in a heavy-based saucepan over medium heat and stir until the sugar has dissolved. Bring to the boil, without stirring, and simmer until the sugar syrup reaches the hard ball stage, 121°C (249°F) on a sugar (candy) thermometer. Alternatively, test by placing a teaspoon of the syrup in cold water, it will form a hard-ball that is still pliable. Remove from the heat.

Beat the gelatine mixture with electric beaters on low speed, then slowly add the hot sugar syrup in a thin steady stream until combined. Increase the speed to medium and beat for a further 8–10 minutes, or until the mixture is sticky, thick, white and fluffy. Working quickly, use a lightly oiled plastic spatula to scrape down the sides of the bowl and tip the mixture into the prepared tin. Smooth the top with the back of a lightly oiled spoon. Allow to stand overnight at room temperature to set.

Combine the icing sugar and cornflour in a bowl. Place a sheet of baking paper on a work surface and sift on just enough icing sugar mixture to cover a 30 cm (12 inch) square. Invert the marshmallow onto the dusted paper and remove the lining paper. Sift on more icing sugar mixture to coat the top surface. Cut the marshmallow into five 20 cm (8 inch) long strips of equal width using a hot knife (dipped in hot water and dried before each cut). Then cut each strip into five squares. Toss the pieces in the remaining icing sugar mixture to coat all sides.

The marshmallow, best eaten fresh, will keep, stored in an airtight container, for up to 1 week.

NOTE: This makes a lovely Christmas gift wrapped in cellophane.

Cranberry, coconut *and* Turkish delight rocky *road*

MAKES *36 pieces*
PREPARATION TIME *35 minutes, plus overnight setting time and chilling time*
COOKING TIME *2 hours*

600 G (1 LB 5 OZ) GOOD-QUALITY *dark chocolate,* ROUGHLY CHOPPED
75 G (2¾ OZ) *sweetened dried cranberries*
75 G (2¾ OZ/1 ¼ CUPS) SHREDDED *coconut,* LIGHTLY TOASTED
100 G (3½ OZ) *macadamia nuts,* TOASTED

Turkish delight

440 G (15½ OZ/2 CUPS) *sugar*
1 TEASPOON *lemon juice*
60 G (2¼ OZ/½ CUP) *cornflour (cornstarch),* PLUS 2 TABLESPOONS EXTRA
½ TEASPOON *cream of tartar*
1 TABLESPOON *rosewater*
4–6 DROPS *red food colouring*
30 G (1 OZ/¼ CUP) *icing (confectioners') sugar*

Spray a 19 cm (7½ inch) square cake tin with oil. Line the base and sides with plastic wrap and lightly spray with oil again.

To make the Turkish delight, place the sugar, 185 ml (6 fl oz/¾ cup) water and the lemon juice in a heavy-based saucepan over medium–high heat and bring to the boil, stirring constantly. Reduce the heat to low and gently simmer, without stirring, for 30–40 minutes, or until the sugar syrup reaches the soft ball stage on a sugar (candy) thermometer 106°C (220°F). (The mixture should be soft and pliable when dropped into cold water and pressed between your finger and thumb.) Remove from the heat. Combine the cornflour and cream of tartar in a large saucepan and whisk in 375 ml (13 fl oz/1½ cups) water until smooth. Place over medium heat and stir constantly until thick. Slowly stir in the sugar syrup. Reduce the heat to low and simmer for 75–80 minutes, or until pale and golden. Stir in the rosewater and food colouring. Pour into the prepared tin and allow to cool, uncovered, at room temperature overnight. Cut into 2 cm (¾ inch) cubes. Sift the icing sugar and extra cornflour onto a plate, add the Turkish delight cubes and toss until well coated.

Spray a 19 cm (7½ inch) square cake tin with oil and line the base and sides with baking paper, extending the paper over two sides for easy removal later. Place the chocolate in a heatproof bowl. Half fill a saucepan with water, bring to the boil and remove from the heat. Sit the bowl over the saucepan, making sure the base of the bowl doesn't touch the water. Stand, stirring occasionally, until the chocolate has melted. Spread one-third of the chocolate into the prepared tin. Scatter evenly with half the cranberries, coconut, macadamia nuts and 250 g (9 oz) of the Turkish delight. Pour over another one-third of the chocolate and scatter on the remaining cranberries, coconut and 250 g (9 oz) of the Turkish delight. Top with the remaining chocolate and tap the tin on the bench. Transfer to the refrigerator to set. Lift out using the paper handles and cut into pieces to serve.

METRO

Pecan shortbread butter *bursts*

MAKES *42*
PREPARATION TIME *30 minutes*
COOKING TIME *10 minutes*

175 G (6 OZ) *butter,* SOFTENED
115 G (4 OZ/½ CUP) *caster (superfine) sugar*
1 TEASPOON *natural vanilla extract*
125 G (4½ OZ/1 CUP) *plain (all-purpose) flour*
45 G (1¾ OZ/¼ CUP) *rice flour*
90 G (3¼ OZ/¾ CUP) *toasted pecans,* FINELY CHOPPED
125 G (4½ OZ/1 CUP) *icing (confectioners') sugar,* SIFTED, FOR DUSTING

Preheat the oven to 180°C (350°F/Gas 4). Line two baking trays with baking paper.

Cream the butter, caster sugar and vanilla in a large bowl using electric beaters until pale and fluffy. Sift in the flours, add the pecans and stir until well combined.

Roll 2 teaspoons of the mixture into balls and place on the prepared trays, leaving room for spreading. Bake for 10 minutes, or until lightly browned. Allow to cool on the trays for 2 minutes and, while still hot, dust with half the icing sugar. Place on wire racks to cool completely. Dust lightly with the remaining icing sugar before serving.

Stained glass biscuit *decorations*

MAKES *25*
PREPARATION TIME *50 minutes, plus 45 minutes chilling time*
COOKING TIME *10 minutes, plus cooling time*

200 G (7 OZ) *unsalted butter,* SOFTENED
100 G (3½ OZ) *icing (confectioners') sugar,* SIFTED
2 *egg yolks*
1 TEASPOON *natural vanilla extract*
300 G (10½ OZ) *plain (all-purpose) flour*
25 *boiled sweets (candy)*
narrow ribbon, TO THREAD

Cream the butter and icing sugar in a large bowl using electric beaters until pale and fluffy. Add the egg yolks one at a time, beating well after each addition. Beat in the vanilla, add the flour and stir until a soft dough forms. Shape the dough into a 2 cm (¾ inch) thick disc, cover with plastic wrap and refrigerate for 30 minutes.

Keeping the colours separate, roughly crush the sweets with a rolling pin and set aside.

Preheat the oven to 180°C (350°F/Gas 4). Line two baking trays with baking paper.

Roll the dough between two sheets of baking paper to 3 mm (⅛ inch) thick. Cut the dough into rounds using a 7 cm (2¾ inch) cutter. Transfer to the prepared trays, then, using 4 cm (1½ inch) Christmas cookie cutters (trees, stars, angels), cut the desired shapes from the centre of each round. Cut a hole in the top of each round about 1 cm (½ inch) from the edge using the end of a straw. Place the trays in the refrigerator for 15 minutes.

Place a teaspoon of the crushed sweets in the cut out sections of each round. Bake for 10 minutes, or until the sweets have melted and the biscuits are pale golden. Allow the biscuits to cool and the 'stained glass' to harden on the trays for 10 minutes. Transfer to a wire rack to cool.

Cut the ribbon into 20 cm (8 inch) lengths, thread through the hole in each biscuit, tie the ends together and hang as Christmas decorations.

Almond biscuits *with* gold leaf

MAKES *40*
PREPARATION TIME *30 minutes, plus 2 hours chilling time*
COOKING TIME *15 minutes, plus cooling time*

125 G ($4\frac{1}{2}$ OZ/$\frac{1}{2}$ CUP) *unsalted butter*
170 G (6 OZ/$\frac{3}{4}$ CUP) *caster (superfine) sugar*
220 G ($7\frac{3}{4}$ OZ/$1\frac{3}{4}$ CUPS) *plain (all-purpose) flour*
$\frac{1}{2}$ TEASPOON FINELY GRATED *lemon zest*
$\frac{1}{2}$ TEASPOON *natural almond extract*
2 *egg yolks*
1 *egg*
1 TABLESPOON *milk*
gold leaf, TO DECORATE

Combine the butter, sugar, flour, lemon zest, almond extract and egg yolks in the bowl of a food processor and pulse until the mixture just comes together to form a dough. Shape the dough into a 2 cm ($\frac{3}{4}$ inch) thick disc and cover with plastic wrap. Refrigerate for 2 hours.

Preheat the oven to 180°C (350°F/Gas 4). Line two baking trays with baking paper.

Divide the dough into 40 even-sized pieces. Roll each piece into a ball and place on the prepared trays.

Whisk the egg and milk in a small bowl and lightly brush the egg wash on top of each ball. Bake for 12–15 minutes, or until golden brown. Allow to cool on the trays for 5 minutes, then transfer to a wire rack to cool completely. Use a toothpick to transfer the gold leaf to the top of each biscuit and gently rub it over the surface.

Walnut *and* chocolate *kisses*

MAKES *35*
PREPARATION TIME *40 minutes, plus 1 hour and 10 minutes chilling time*
COOKING TIME *10 minutes, plus cooling time*

125 G (4½ OZ/1¼ CUPS) *walnut halves*
220 G (7¾ OZ) *plain (all-purpose) flour*
115 G (4 OZ/½ CUP) *caster (superfine) sugar*
125 G (4½ OZ/½ CUP) *unsalted butter,* CHILLED AND CUT INTO CUBES
1 *egg yolk*

Ganache filling

60 ML (2 FL OZ/¼ CUP) *cream*
120 G (4¼ OZ) *dark chocolate* (70 PER CENT COCOA SOLIDS), CHOPPED

Topping

180 G (6¼ OZ) *dark chocolate* (70 PER CENT COCOA SOLIDS), CHOPPED
35 *walnut halves*

Place the walnuts in the bowl of a food processor and process until the consistency of breadcrumbs. Add the flour and sugar and pulse to mix well. Add the butter and egg yolk and pulse until the mixture just comes together to form a dough. Turn the dough out onto a lightly floured work surface and form into a disc. Cover with plastic wrap and refrigerate for 1 hour.

Preheat the oven to 180°C (350°F/Gas 4). Line two baking trays with baking paper.

Roll out the dough on a lightly floured work surface to form a 20 x 30 cm (8 x 12 inch) rectangle. Cut out 70 rounds using a 3 cm (1¼ inch) cutter, gathering the dough scraps together and re-rolling, as required. Place the rounds 4 cm (1½ inches) apart on the prepared trays and refrigerate for 10 minutes. Bake for 8 minutes, or until the bases are golden. Allow to cool on the trays for 5 minutes, then transfer to a wire rack to cool.

To make the ganache filling, place the cream in a small saucepan and bring to a simmer. Remove from the heat, add the chocolate and set aside, stirring occasionally, until the chocolate has melted. Allow to cool to room temperature. The mixture will be thick, smooth and easy to spread.

Meanwhile, to make the topping, place the chocolate in a small heatproof bowl. Half fill a small saucepan with water, bring to the boil and remove from the heat. Sit the bowl over the saucepan, making sure the base of the bowl doesn't touch the water. Stir occasionally, until the chocolate has melted. Using a small palette knife, spread the chocolate on half the biscuits, leaving a 2 mm (1/16 inch) border around the edge, then top with a walnut. Allow to set.

Spread the base of each remaining biscuit with the ganache filling and sandwich together with a choc-walnut topped biscuit.

Panforte

SERVES *10–12*
PREPARATION TIME *20 minutes*
COOKING TIME *40 minutes, plus cooling time*

100 G (3½ OZ/⅔ CUP) BLANCHED *almonds*
105 G (3½ OZ/¾ CUP) *hazelnuts,* TOASTED AND SKINNED
95 G (3¼ OZ/½ CUP) *mixed peel (mixed candied citrus peel),* CHOPPED
110 G (3¾ OZ/½ CUP) CHOPPED *glacé (candied) pineapple*
30 G (1 OZ/¼ CUP) *unsweetened cocoa powder*
60 G (2¼ OZ/½ CUP) *plain (all-purpose) flour*
½ TEASPOON *ground cinnamon*
¼ TEASPOON *mixed (pumpkin pie) spice*
75 G (2¾ OZ/⅓ CUP) *sugar*
115 G (4 OZ/⅓ CUP) *honey*
icing (confectioners') sugar, SIFTED, FOR DUSTING

Grease and line a 20 cm (8 inch) spring-form cake tin with baking paper.

Toast the almonds under a hot grill (broiler) until golden, then set aside to cool. Place the almonds and hazelnuts in a heatproof bowl, add the mixed peel, pineapple, cocoa, flour and spices and toss well.

Preheat the oven to 150°C (300°F/Gas 2).

Combine the sugar and honey in a small heavy-based saucepan and cook over low heat until the sugar dissolves. Continue to cook until the syrup reaches the soft ball stage (the mixture should be soft and pliable when dropped into cold water and pressed between your finger and thumb) and turns from golden to brown in colour.

Pour the syrup onto the nut mixture and, working quickly, mix well before it hardens. Spoon into the prepared tin, pressing down firmly, and smooth the surface. Bake for 35 minutes. Unlike other cakes this will neither firm up nor colour as it cooks, so you need to time it carefully.

Cool in the tin until the cake is firm enough to allow you to remove the side of the tin. Peel off the lining paper, and set aside to cool completely. Dust the top heavily with the icing sugar before serving.

NOTE: This fruity, spicy, dense-textured flat cake originated in Siena, Tuscany. It can be stored, wrapped in baking paper and foil and refrigerated, for up to 6 weeks.

Gingerbread *stars*

MAKES *48*
PREPARATION TIME *40 minutes, plus 30 minutes chilling time*
COOKING TIME *10 minutes*

150 G (5½ OZ) *butter,* SOFTENED
115 G (4 OZ/½ CUP) *caster (superfine) sugar*
3 TABLESPOONS *honey*
1 *egg*
340 G (11¾ OZ/2¾ CUPS) *plain (all-purpose) flour*
½ TEASPOON *baking powder*
1 TEASPOON *bicarbonate of soda (baking soda)*
1 TEASPOON *ground cinnamon*
1 TABLESPOON *ground ginger*
silver cachous, TO DECORATE

Glacé icing

185 G (6½ OZ/1½ CUPS) *icing (confectioners') sugar*
½ TEASPOON SOFTENED *butter*
2–2½ TABLESPOONS *boiling water*

Royal icing

1 *egg white*
185 G (6½ OZ/1½ CUPS) *icing (confectioners') sugar*
½–1 TEASPOON *lemon juice*

Cream the butter, sugar and honey in a large bowl using electric beaters until pale and fluffy. Add the egg and beat well. Sift in the flour, baking powder, bicarbonate of soda, cinnamon and ginger and stir until the mixture comes together to form a ball. Turn out onto a lightly floured work surface and gently knead until smooth. Cover with plastic wrap and refrigerate for 30 minutes.

Preheat the oven to 180°C (350°F/Gas 4). Line two baking trays with baking paper.

Roll out the dough on a lightly floured work surface to 2 mm (1/16 inch) thick. Cut the dough into star shapes with a 7 cm (2¾ inch) star-shaped cookie cutter, re-rolling any dough scraps and cutting out more stars. Place on the prepared trays, leaving room for a little spreading, and bake for 6 minutes, or until lightly browned. Allow to cool on the trays for 2 minutes, then transfer to a wire rack to cool completely.

To make the glacé icing, combine the icing sugar, butter and water in a small heatproof bowl and mix to a smooth paste. Place the bowl over a saucepan of simmering water and stir until warm and the consistency of whipping cream. Do not overheat. Dip the top of each star into the icing and allow the excess to drip off. Leave on a wire rack to set.

To make the royal icing, lightly whisk the egg white in a small bowl until just foamy. Gradually whisk in enough icing sugar and lemon juice to form a smooth icing that holds its shape. Spoon the icing into a piping (icing) bag fitted with a small 2 mm (1/16 inch) plain nozzle (or use a zip-lock bag and snip off a small corner) and pipe decorations onto the gingerbread stars. Decorate with silver cachous if desired. Allow to set.

Chocolate fruit mince *tarts*

MAKES *24*
PREPARATION TIME *1 hour, plus 2 days soaking time and 35 minutes chilling time*
COOKING TIME *20 minutes, plus cooling time*

125 G (4½ OZ/½ CUP) *unsalted butter,* CHILLED AND CUT INTO CUBES
155 G (5½ OZ/1¼ CUPS) *plain (all-purpose) flour*
2 TABLESPOONS *unsweetened cocoa powder*
55 G (2 OZ) *icing (confectioners') sugar,* SIFTED, PLUS EXTRA FOR DUSTING
1 *egg yolk*
½ TABLESPOON *iced water*

Filling

400 G (14 OZ) *mixed dried fruit*
50 G (1¾ OZ/⅓ CUP) BLANCHED *almonds,* CHOPPED
55 G (2 OZ/¼ CUP) *soft brown sugar*
½ TEASPOON *mixed (pumpkin pie) spice*
½ TEASPOON *ground ginger*
1 *medium granny smith apple,* PEELED AND COARSELY GRATED
1 TEASPOON FINELY GRATED *orange zest*
1 TEASPOON FINELY GRATED *lemon zest*
2 TABLESPOONS *orange juice*
1 TABLESPOON *lemon juice*
125 G (4½ OZ) GOOD-QUALITY *dark chocolate,* FINELY CHOPPED
30 G (1 OZ) *unsalted butter,* MELTED
2 TABLESPOONS *brandy*

To make the filling, combine all the ingredients in a bowl, mix well, then spoon into a sterilised jar and seal. Set aside for at least 2 days to allow the fruit mince to develop.

Place the butter, flour and cocoa in the bowl of a food processor and process until the consistency of fine breadcrumbs. Add the sugar and egg yolk and pulse until the dough just comes together, adding the water, if necessary. Turn the dough out onto a lightly floured work surface and gather into a ball. Cover in plastic wrap and refrigerate for 30 minutes.

Preheat the oven to 180°C (350°F/Gas 4). Lightly grease two 12-hole mini muffin tins.

Slice the pastry in half. Place one piece between two sheets of baking paper and roll out to 2 mm (1/16 inch) thick, scattering with flour where necessary. Cut out 24 rounds from the pastry using a 7 cm (2¾ inch) cutter. Line the prepared tins with the pastry, trim off any excess and set aside for decorating. Prick the bases with a fork and place in the freezer for 5 minutes.

Divide the fruit mince filling among the pastry cases, ensuring that each case is heaped with the filling.

Roll out the remaining pastry until very thin and cut into strips. Brush the ends of each strip with water and arrange in a cross over each tart. Bake for 15–20 minutes, or until the pastry is crisp and golden. Allow to cool in the tins for 5 minutes, then lift out with a knife and cool on wire racks. Dust lightly with the icing sugar.

NOTE: The fruit mince will keep, stored in a cool dark place, for up to 3 months.

Index

D

E

F

G

H

I

J

L

M

Previously published as Cooking for Christmas in 2009.
This edition published in 2026 by Murdoch Books, an imprint of Allen & Unwin.

Murdoch Books Australia
Cammeraygal Country
83 Alexander Street
Crows Nest NSW 2065
Phone: +61 (0)2 8425 0100
murdochbooks.com.au
info@murdochbooks.com.au

Murdoch Books UK
Ormond House
26–27 Boswell Street
London WC1N 3JZ
Phone: +44 (0) 20 8785 5995
murdochbooks.co.uk
info@murdochbooks.co.uk

For corporate orders and custom publishing, contact our business development team at salesenquiries@murdochbooks.com.au

Publisher (this edition): Justin Wolfers
Project editor: Livia Caiazzo
Designers: Vivien Valk and Erika Cvejic
Designer (this edition): Sharon Misko
Photographer: George Seper
Stylist: Sarah O'Brien
Food editor: Chrissy Freer
Copy editor: Megan Johnston
Production manager: Natalie Crouch

Murdoch Books acknowledges the Traditional Owners of the Country on which we live and work. We pay our respects to all Aboriginal and Torres Strait Islander Elders, past and present.

Our authorised representative in the EU for product safety is Easy Access System Europe, Mustamäe tee 50, 10621 Tallinn, Estonia, gpsr.requests@easproject.com

ISBN 978 1 76150 137 1

NATIONAL LIBRARY OF AUSTRALIA
A catalogue record for this book is available from the National Library of Australia

A catalogue record for this book is available from the British Library

Colour reproduction by Splitting Image Colour Studio Pty Ltd, Wantirna, Victoria
Printed in China by 1010 Printing International Limited, China

OVEN GUIDE: You may find cooking times vary depending on the oven and oven setting you are using. For fan-forced (convection) ovens, as a general rule, set the oven temperature to 20°C (25–50°F) lower than indicated in the recipe.

TABLESPOON MEASURES: We have used 20 ml (4 teaspoon) tablespoon measures. If you are using a 15 ml (3 teaspoon) tablespoon add an extra teaspoon of the ingredient for each tablespoon specified.

IMPORTANT: Those who might be at risk from the effects of salmonella poisoning (the elderly, pregnant women, young children and those suffering from immune deficiency diseases) should consult their doctor with any concerns about eating raw eggs.

10 9 8 7 6 5 4 3 2 1

FSC www.fsc.org MIX Paper | Supporting responsible forestry FSC® C016973